How Will We Live Then:
What Lies Ahead After This Life?

By Paul Scheperle

How Will We Live Then: What Lies Ahead After This Life?

Printed by Lulu.com

Copyright © 2010 by Paul A. Scheperle

Washington, MO USA
All rights reserved

Unless otherwise noted, all Scripture quotations are taken from the NEW INTERNATIONAL VERSION® [niv]. Copyright © 1973, 1978, 1984 by International Bible Society. Used by permission of Zondervan Publishing House.

Cataloguing Data
Scheperle, Paul A., 1971-
How Shall We Live Then

Hard Cover ISBN 978-0-557-31459-1
Paperback ISBN 978-0-557-31955-8

1. Bible - Theology. 2. Heaven

Dedicated to my family, who allowed me the time to write.

Special thanks to the church I pastor, for their encouragement to keep going.

Table of Contents

Introduction • 7

1. "I do not want you to be ignorant" • 13
   What happens to Christians when they die?

2. Decomposition Re-Commissioned • 29
   The resurrection of believers

3. Going, Going, Gone • 39
   The rapture of the church

4. Celebrate! Celebrate! • 53
   The marriage supper of the lamb

5. Riding in the Clouds • 69
   The believers' part in Jesus' second coming

6. "The meek shall inherit the earth" • 83
   The believers part in the millennium

7. Forever • 99
   Living in eternity

Conclusion • 113

How Will We Live Then?

Introduction

What drives your life? Is there some thing that really motivates you to action in life? For many of us, we are driven by our jobs, the need for money or the prospect of wealth. For some of us, our driving force is our family. We love our spouse, children and parents, and that love drives us to action. For some people, the driving force in their life is a hobby. They live for the weekend and the opportunity to engage in a certain activity again. Whatever you love, enjoy or cherish most, that is the driving force in your life. For many people, a love for Christ drives and motivates their life and affects every decision they make.

If you are a Christian think back for a moment, what drove you to accept the Lord? For many Christians the motivation to accept Christ, serve the Lord, and be a witness is the fear of hell. Obviously this is a God inspired Biblical motivation. Proverbs 1:7 says, "The fear of the Lord is the beginning of knowledge." Hell and The Lake of Fire are places that are listed in the Bible as literal locations of extreme, permanent suffering. Jesus taught about hell. That teaching is intended to instill respect for the Lord.

Many Christians serve the Lord to avoid hell. They are in Christ because they fear the consequences of life without Christ. There is a very distinct problem in the life of a believer who is motivated by fear of hell *only*. There is a more pleasant, and equally powerful, motivator! The other motivator that God gives us is the promise of heaven! As much as we fear hell we need to long for heaven and the promise of spending eternity with the Lord.

Let me list a few specific problems with fear driven motivation. First, fear driven motivation will only do what is necessary to get by. A Christian motivated by fear of hell will always ask the question, "What is the minimum I must do to avoid hell?" The fear motivated Christian will struggle between wanting more of God and the lack of motivation to go get it. If the minimum requirement to avoid hell is met, what motivation is there to seek more of God unless there is a catastrophe in life? Often these believers find themselves fearful all over again because of a sermon or book and will rededicate their life and strive for God for a while. However, when the feeling of fear wears off, old habits of lethargy return.

Second, the fear motivated Christian will have a negative oriented witness. You will only witness what you really know in your heart. If your heart is driven by fear, then your witness will be driven by fear. You will witness because you are fearful for yourself. You fear God's displeasure so much that you will grit your teeth and tell someone about Jesus. Not only will your internal feeling about witnessing be negative; your witness will be negative in its orientation. We need to tell people about hell, but I also want to tell them about God's love and his awesome promise of heaven. Which would you rather highlight in your witness? "You are a sinner going to hell," or "Jesus loves you and will prepare a place for you in heaven if you will accept him today."

Third, the fear motivated Christian will be stunted in their spiritual growth. What is spiritual growth really? It is loving, serving and knowing Jesus better. I don't want anything to keep me from growing spiritually. However, many of us have been caught in the trap of growing because of fear only. Jesus was asked, "What is the greatest commandment?" His response was "Love the Lord your God." Interestingly, though fear of the Lord is commended in Scripture, his response was not fear the Lord. His response was not to submit to the Lord, though loving the Lord means absolute submission to him. God's desire is that we love him and that our love for him will drive us to be more like him and spend our time with him and for him.

While many Christians serve the Lord because they fear the wrath of God, there is another false motivator that drives many to serve the Lord. Many people have come to the Lord because of a need or a want that they believed God would meet. We serve a prayer answering God! He will bless us and make us prosper so that we will be able to have more than we need and give to others (2 Cor. 9:1-11). However, if we are serving the Lord because we think that it will make us rich, successful, happy or give us an easy life, we are confused about God's eternal plan for us.

Jesus said, "In this world you will have trouble." What will be our fate if we are driven by earthly success and instead we get trouble? Many fallen friends line the edges of the narrow path disappointed that God did not give them what they wanted, when they wanted it. Our driving force and motivation has to be able to bring us through the suffering of this life. Paul said in 1 Corinthians 15:19, "If only for this life we have hope in Christ, we are pitied more than all men."

Our driving force to serve the Lord has many facets. We reverently fear the Lord. We have faith that he will bless us in this life. Most of all, as we serve him and seek him, we fall in love with him and are driven by his love. The Bible gives several motivators for serving the Lord, but there is one that we are allowing to fall by the wayside. We have lost the motivation of heaven and eternal life with him.

How do we know that we have lost the driving force of heaven? First, look in any old hymnal. The majority of songs have a verse about heaven, or the entire song is about heaven. Now, think about all the songs you sang at church on Sunday. Which one was about heaven? I know that there are some exceptions, but most of our worship music has left out heaven in the last ten years. One of the most popular songs in recent years has been *I Can Only Imagine*. Why was it so popular? It filled a drastic heaven void in the Christian music industry.

Second, look at the most recent books on Bible prophecy and the most recent sermon series you have heard on the end times. The great bulk of that teaching was probably spent on the Antichrist, the Beast, the Dragon, the Four Horsemen, the Seven Seals, Trumpets, and Bowls of Wrath and other kinds of horrible events. They are surely coming. God's word is true. However, how much of that teaching was spent in 1 Corinthians 15, 1 Thessalonians 4, Revelation 4-5, or Revelation 19-22? While the world is experiencing God's judgment, what will we be doing as Christians? We have lost the motivation of the resurrection of believers, the wedding supper of the Lamb, the armies of heaven returning with the Lord, ruling and reigning with Jesus, and the restoration of all things in the new heaven and the new earth.

Third, consider the nature of our preaching that is driving us to be comfortable and tolerant in this world. Our preaching is driving us to be politically powerful in this world rather than in the next! Our preaching drives us to be successful now, using the world's standards of success. Remember when Paul's followers began to evaluate his success using worldly standards? He wrote 2 Corinthians in response to those evaluations. First, he chided them in 10:7 saying, "You are looking only on the surface of things." Then Paul boasted, "I have worked harder, been in prison more frequently, been flogged more severely…" Paul's boasting was not in miracles, numbers of converts, or financial solvency of his ministry. Paul boasted in the fact that he was stirring up the world for Christ and the proof was persecution. Paul underwent such difficulty because he loved his Lord and because, in his own words, "Now there is in store for me the crown of righteousness, which the Lord, the righteous judge, will award to me on that day…"

Fourth, we have lost sight of heaven because life has become so easy. One hundred years ago Christians longed for heaven because they had no air conditioning, no clean car to ride in, no amusement park or Christian concert to escape to, and no TV to vegetate with. There were no miracle surgeries or wonder drugs. Infant mortality was high and the average life was shorter. If you visit the third world, you will find the same scene. When life is stagnant and rotten, water from the river of life tastes better. When life stinks the fruit of the tree of life smells sweeter. A very successful lawyer friend once told me, "God has blessed me so much I have to remind myself that this is not heaven once in a while." Yes, we certainly need to remind ourselves that this is not heaven. We must be careful about becoming so proud of *our* world with all its amenities that we loose sight of the new world that we will inherit when Jesus comes again.

So, what is driving you? When you search your heart, what really motivates you to love the Lord and minister for him? There are many motivators in the Scriptures, but have you lost the motivation of heaven and eternity with Christ? My hope is that in reading these words that you will long to understand more about what the Bible says about your great future in eternity.

Chapter 1
"I do not want you to be ignorant"
What happens to Christians when they die?

One of the most common questions answered by any world view, religion, or culture is, "What happens when we die?" In the movie, *It's a Wonderful Life*, staring Jimmy Stewart, the guardian angel Clarence is trying to earn his wings. Clarence was a man who had lived on earth, died and went to heaven. We meet Clarence in the next step in his existence, trying to earn his wings and become a first class angel. Zuzu hears a bell ring at the end of the movie and says, "Every time a bell rings an angel gets its wings." We assume that Clarence just moved up in rank and earned his wings.

Though many people actually believe that they become angels when they get to heaven, this is clearly not taught by the Bible at all. On the other hand, many people, even some who claim to be Christians, have a dark and morbid view of death. The Bible says, *"Precious in the sight of the Lord is the death of his saints."*[1]

Death is precious and a beautiful transition for a believer. So, what really happens when a follower of Christ dies?

You need to understand one thing before examining life after death. A Christian should never fear death. The fear of death is only the fear of the unknown. If we know that heaven awaits us then what is there to fear? If you doubt that you are on your way to heaven, you ought to be fearful. You can be and need to be saved. Ask Jesus to forgive your sins and direct your life by the Word and Spirit of God. Stop reading right now and pray. God loves you and wants to forgive you right now!

The Bogus Suspicions

> *"Brothers, we do not want you to be ignorant about those who fall asleep, or to grieve like the rest of men, who have no hope." 1 Thessalonians 4:13*

The purpose of Paul's writing to the Thessalonians was that they would not be ignorant. Ignorant does not mean stupid or lacking intelligence, but it refers to lacking information. Many people lack information regarding the promises of God for our future existence. That lack of information is due to the deficiencies that we discussed in the introduction. Ignorance, bogus suspicions, myths and fairy tales have emerged in this information vacuum. Let's look at some the bogus suspicions that are popular today.

We Cease to Exist

Perhaps the most popular opinion today is that we cease to exist at death. We are no more than a tree or a plant. If this is the end result of a life lived on earth, then the only logical way to live is some form of hedonism. We must attempt to achieve the greatest amount of happiness for the greatest number of people for the longest amount of time. Of course, Friedrich Nietzsche in the 1800's and the Nazis in the 20th century wanted to secure this form of happiness and were willing to go to extreme measures. They thought the powerful, intelligent and rich must create happiness for the masses, even if it involves violent means. Ultimately, if we take this philosophical naturalist view we live as if there is no God, no reward or punishment for this life, and we are not accountable beyond society, or beyond this life for anything we choose to do.

Jesus confronted this bogus suspicion in the Scriptures when he encountered the Sadducees. There were two sects in Judaism in first century Palestine where Jesus lived. The Pharisees believed in an afterlife, the Sadducees did not[2]. A Bible college professor used to teach us to remember this by saying, "They were *sad you see*, because they did not believe in life after death." By looking at Jesus' interaction with this sect we find information about what Jesus believed about heaven.

In Matthew 22 the Sadducees asked Jesus a question about life after death to test him. They obviously did not believe in life after death. First Jesus reprimands them for not knowing the Old Testament Scriptures properly, "*You are in error because you do not know the Scriptures or the power of God.*" Then Jesus goes on to explain how life will be after death. Then Jesus quotes Exodus 3:6, *I am the God of Abraham, the God of Isaac, and the God of Jacob…*" indicating that God is currently, the God of individuals who died thousands of years before. Then

Jesus says, *"He is not the God of the dead but of the living."* From Jesus' rebuke of those of his day who did not believe in an afterlife, we can know that Jesus Christ did not believe that people cease to exist after death.

Everyone Goes to Heaven

Another popular opinion today believes there is an afterlife. There is an actual heaven just as the Bible teaches, and everyone is going there. There are all kinds of versions of this thinking. Formally, there are theologians who believe in universal salvation, the idea that because Jesus died for everyone, that everyone will go to heaven regardless of their life on earth. Other forms of universal salvation assert that those who arrive in hell find it horrible and very quickly repent and are saved out of hell. More commonly, people today just assume that when anyone dies that they go to "a better place."

Jesus did not teach this bogus suspicion. In Matthew 7:13-14, Jesus said that the way to life was a narrow road and few find it. In Matthew 22 Jesus says, *"many are invited but few are chosen."* So first we see that not everyone will find or choose the life Jesus offers. But what if they can choose after they die? Again, in Matthew 22, the parable of the wedding banquet, we find a wedding crasher at the party. The host throws them out. You can not squeak into heaven by a route other than the one presented to you today by Jesus. Also in the parable of the ten virgins in Matthew 25, the virgins who missed the initial opportunity to enter the party were not given access when they tried to get in later. As the proverb says, *"Whether a tree falls to the south or to the north, in the place where it falls, there will it lie."* What we choose to do with Jesus Christ in this life determines our destiny in eternity.

We Will Become Angels

This is the idea that is illustrated in the movie we mentioned before, *It's A Wonderful Life*. This is a notion that we become something different when we die. Actually, it is encouraging to note that God created mankind in the Garden of Eden *"very good."*[3] Man was perfect in the garden and the purpose of God's salvation plan is to bring us back to that state of perfection. God did not send man out of the garden because he was mad and mean, but because he wants us to be perfect.

> [22]*And the LORD God said, "The man has now become like one of us, knowing good and evil. He must not be allowed to reach out his hand and take also from the tree of life and eat, and live forever."* [23] *So the LORD God banished him from the Garden of Eden to work the ground from which he had been taken.* [24] *After he drove the man out, he placed on the east side of the Garden of Eden cherubim and a flaming sword flashing back and forth to guard the way to the tree of life.*[4]

So, God sent man out of the garden, not out of vengeance but out of a desire to make man perfect again. God has no desire to allow you to live forever in a state of sinfulness. God is not making us into angels, but into perfect people. Furthermore, God already had angels. Notice that when the humans were sent out of the garden that an angel guarded the way back into the garden.

It is also important to note that the angels currently in heaven were never humans. In 1 Peter 1:11-12 Peter is explaining the amazing interaction between three things: humans preaching of the Gospel, the work of the Holy Spirit, and the resulting salvation of individuals. At least three persons all involved in the salvation of one person, a human spokesperson used by God, the Holy Sprit of God working in both, and the one being saved. Then Peter makes a side note, *"Even angels long to look into these things."* Angels were never human, and they watch with interest our interaction with God.

We Will Be Unconscious for a While

Some groups call this idea soul sleep. It is the idea that at death we go into an unconscious state and then God wakes us back up at some later time. The unconscious person does not even register time passing. In the Scriptures, Paul writes that those who have died in the Lord are asleep[5]. Based on this wording, some have assumed that the soul is unconscious after death waiting to be awakened at the resurrection. As we shall see in future chapters, we are not unconscious after we die, we are busy enjoying great things.

We Will Be Wandering Ghosts

Many people believe that there are intermediary places that we must pass through first. In pop culture and in movies it is popular to believe that the spirits of people roam the earth trying to finish business left undone in life. Movies like *The Sixth Sense* make this idea seem realistic. Ghost stories add to that drama and the questions that people have about death.

There are places in Scripture where the spirits of the dead are in contact with the living. In 1 Samuel 28, King Saul had a medium call up the spirit of Samuel, the prophet. This story is one of the great failures of Saul. The Scriptures prohibit the children of God from consulting mediums and fortune tellers or any other spirits for direction. God is so jealous for a relationship with us that he does not want us seeking or praying to the spirits or souls of any other entities. We trust in the Lord, not in deceased saints (saints are not dead, they are with the Lord). The difficulty with this passage is that we are not told how it was that the medium had the authority to call up Samuel. What is important is that Saul's contact with the dead was displeasing to God.

The other place where we find the dead in contact with the living is at the transfiguration. In that instance, God sent Moses and Elijah to meet with Jesus. We don't know what they discussed and we don't know all the extent of what God accomplished at that time. We do know that Jesus was glorified in the presence of his Father and we assume he was encouraged by the meeting with Moses and Elijah.

The Brief Separation

One of the most common questions that I am asked as a pastor is, "What happens when we die?" It is almost always asked at funerals. The question is asked at almost every meeting I have had with a family who lost a loved one and had to make funeral arrangements. Amazingly, it is asked by Christians and non-Christians alike. Christians need to know what happens when they die. The Bible does not tell us all the mechanical details. However, the Scriptures tell us enough that we do not need to be ignorant or grieve like people who have no knowledge of the hope of heaven.[6]

Second Corinthians gives us a basic principle explaining what believers will be like immediately after death.

> *Therefore we are always confident and know that as long as we are at home in the body we are away from the Lord. ⁷We live by faith and not by sight. We are confident, I say, and would prefer to be away from the body and at home with the Lord. So we make it our goal to please him, whether we are at home in the body or away from it."*[7]

Humans are created by God with a complex nature. We are individuals, but made up of parts that can be separated without making us separate individuals. Each person is made up of a physical body, a spirit, a mind and a soul.[8] When believers die, the body begins to decompose; but the soul, mind, and spirit continue on, and the spirit and mind become even better!

When a person is saved their soul is saved. The picture of the blood being applied to the doorframes of Israelite homes in Exodus 12:7 at Passover helps us see this. The blood of Jesus is applied to the soul of a believer. But the human spirit, mind and body are still flawed by sin and capable of error. A person can be saved, growing in the Lord and have needs in their mind, body and spirit. A Christian must *"not conform any longer to the pattern of this world, but be transformed by the renewing of your mind."*[9] We need to *"be made new in the attitude of our minds."*[10] Obviously, our minds need some work though our soul is spotless before God, covered by Jesus' precious blood.

Consider the spirit. The Bible says the Word of God is powerful. *"It penetrates even to dividing soul and spirit"*[11] The word of God can separate soul and spirit in making judgments about right and wrong. The soul is saved, but the word of God points out the errors of the human spirit; thus the two are divided by the word of God, though they are intertwined beyond our ability to understand completely. *"The spirits of prophets are subject to the control of prophets,"*[12] that is, they need accountability and direction. They are not perfect. The Bible also says, *"do not believe every spirit, but test the spirits to see whether they are from God."*[13] If spirits need to be tested, what spirits are they? Some are evil spirits and some are human spirits. Evil spirits are always wrong, and human spirits can be wrong and are sometimes misguided.

Our bodies are not perfect. Bodies grow old, get weak, sick and all eventually die. God has a plan for your body. God has saved your soul. He is saving your spirit, mind and body; and some day they will be completely redeemed as well. The discussion about the effect of salvation on the human body is yet to come.

One of my favorite parts of the committal service is when the minister stands next to the casket of the dead at the cemetery and says that the deceased "is not here." When you attend a funeral, realize that the person has left their body behind. The believer has gone on to be with the Lord. The conclusion is this. When a believer dies, the body is separated from the soul, mind and spirit. The consciousness, memory and spiritual nature of believers are with the Lord. But where is that?

The Beautiful Situation

Once believers have left their bodies and have gone on to be with the Lord, where are they and what are the conditions of the place in which they exist? There are, again, many suspicions that have been suggested, but our goal is to find out the Bible truth. First, it is important to note from 2 Corinthians 5 that when Christians die they go to be present with the Lord. That clears up many misconceptions about intermediate locations and states between our earthly life and being with the Lord.

Many believe, because their denomination teaches them the doctrine of purgatory, that after death they are not present with the Lord, but must pay the remaining sin debts that were not confessed in life. The doctrine of purgatory is not in the scriptures at all. It is an extrapolation. What I mean is this, if your church teaches that baptism saves the individual, then they must be saved and on their way to heaven. But, the traditional doctrine of the Roman Catholic Church is also that sin must be confessed and penance performed for forgiveness to be achieved. What about unconfessed sins at death? The individual is saved, but cannot enter heaven with unforgiven sin. Thus, there must be an intermediary place where sins will be atoned for. In the middle ages, it was customary for the church to teach that Purgatory was a temporary hell, a place of flaming torment. The tradition of the Catholic doctrine has been to teach that Purgatory is a place of temporary pain and punishment like Hell, lasting anywhere from a few years to tens of thousands of years. Individuals in these churches are encouraged to pray for their friends and relatives after they have died. They are praying that God would receive them, supposedly out of purgatory. If you read the Catholic Catechism that was edited by Joseph Ratzinger, who is now Pope Benedict, you will see that indulgences are still available for penance. To think that the medieval teaching of purgatory and indulgences has disappeared, is incorrect.[14]

This is obviously not the case according to the apostle Paul. His personal anticipation was that upon his death, and the death of other believers, they would be in the presence of the Lord. I am often asked to pray for the dead, but I do not do it. It is a wonderful opportunity to show Christians that when a believer in Jesus Christ dies, they go to Heaven to be with the Lord. It is an opportunity to explain that Jesus paid the full price for our sins and that we are not required, nor able, to do penance for those sins to be removed. It makes the work of Jesus so much more amazing when we think about the great grace of God to forgive, the power of our relationship with him and our standing with him as the children of God.

We have noted then, that when Christians die, they go to be with the Lord. But where is that? The second part of the situation that the Bible describes is the location. Because we are limited to earth at this time, we can not know, or perhaps even understand, the location of Heaven as it exists right now. Here is what we do know:
One, when Jesus left the earth, the Bible says he went to Heaven. *"This same Jesus who has been taken from you into Heaven, will come back in the same way you have seen him go into Heaven."*[15] Also, in Acts 7:56, Stephen saw heaven opened when he was being stoned and Jesus was standing to receive him. The Bible indicates that to be present with the Lord is to be in Heaven. (Later we will see that Heaven will be re-made for our eternal home.)

There is not a clear description of the current state of Heaven in the Bible. There is far more description of the New Heaven, the New Earth and the New

Jerusalem. We will discuss this later in the book. That is when we will experience the streets of gold and the pearly gates and those amazing images of Heaven. Perhaps the best descriptions of Heaven in its current state are in Revelation chapters 4 and 19. John was shown the throne room of God in these passages. What we know for sure is that it is amazing, it is huge in proportions, and that God is present there in amazing glory. God is everywhere, but he does not reveal all of his glory in all places the same way. Also, it seems apparent from Revelation 19 that those in Heaven can observe the events or know about the events on Earth. The inhabitants of Heaven have been aware of the things that have transpired on Earth.[16]

One of the main goals of this book is to describe what the Bible says we as believers will be like in the future. Let's look at a few quick points that show us what believers in heaven are like right now. What will we be like if we are with him at this time? First, we will know each other. In Luke 16, Jesus tells a story that is similar to a parable, but in its wording he indicates that it is a true story about a rich man and Lazarus the beggar. In that story, Jesus indicates that the individuals who have died recognize each other. *"In hell, where he was in torment, he looked up and saw Abraham far away, with Lazarus by his side."*[17] One of the great blessings of Heaven will be that we will recognize each other. We will be united with friends and family that have gone on to Heaven before us. This reinforces the truth that we are made for relationship, not only with God, but with others.

The second thing we can know about heaven as it exists right now is that we will have a fully renewed mind. Our minds are not perfect, as we noted in the beginning of this chapter. But the Bible has a great promise for us. *"Now we see but a poor reflection as in a mirror; then we shall see face to face. Now I know in part; then I shall know fully, even as I am fully known." 1 Corinthians 13:12.* The mind is completely renewed when a believer dies and is in the presence of the Lord.

Third, we will have rest. The writer of Hebrews understood that one of the promises of Heaven is rest. Hebrews 4:8-9 sasy, *"⁸For if Joshua had given them rest, God would not have spoken later about another day. ⁹There remains, then, a Sabbath-rest for the people of God."*

Fourth, we will be united with followers of Christ. Read what the book of Revelation says about Christians in Heaven.

> *"⁹After this I looked and there before me was a great multitude that no one could count, from every nation, tribe, people and language, standing before the throne and in front of the Lamb. They were wearing white robes and were holding palm branches in their hands. ¹⁰And they cried out in a loud voice: "Salvation belongs to our God, who sits on the throne, and to the Lamb."*[18]

The picture in Revelation seven is of believers after their resurrection. It is a glimpse into the joy of being reunited with other believers when we go on to be with the Lord. Again, drawing from the story of the rich man and Lazarus, we find believers associating in Abraham's bosom, the place where Old Testament believers went after their deaths. It was a pleasant place, where they waited until Jesus had finished his redeeming work on the cross. We don't really know that much about that location. What is interesting is that Abraham, one of the most important and greatest figures of the Bible, is hanging out with Lazarus. Lazarus is a Scriptural nobody who received no attention in life, but Jesus tells his unknown story postmortem. We will be united with other followers of Jesus when we die and go to heaven. That includes people we have been close to in life, our believing ancestors, and the saints of the Scriptures. I am looking forward to meeting the Scheperles who were early Lutherans. Our family tree has been traced to the 1540s' through church baptismal records in Lutheran churches in Germany. It is neat to think that I have ancestors who were concerned about their condition before God and were first generation Protestant believers.

Fifth, we will wait for the redemption of our bodies. Romans 8:23 says, *"Not only so, but we ourselves, who have the first fruits of the Spirit, groan inwardly as we wait eagerly for our adoption as sons, the redemption of our bodies."* Presently, our bodies, spirits and minds are in the process of being saved. Our full salvation has not been revealed. Our minds and spirits will be fully redeemed at death, but we will still be waiting for the resurrection of our bodies.

Sixth, we will be waiting to fully rule and reign with him. Revelation 20:6 says, *"Blessed and holy are those who have part in the first resurrection. The second death has no power over them, but they will be priests of God and of Christ and will reign with him for a thousand years."* Since we have already been judged regarding our acceptance into Heaven at the time of our death, we will be secured in the resurrection and our part in the millennial reign of Christ which includes the reward of ruling and reigning with Christ.

Seventh, we will celebrate! John 16:22 says, *"So with you: Now is your time of grief, but I will see you again and you will **rejoice**, and no one will take away your joy."* We will first see the Lord after we have died, unless he returns in our lifetime and we are caught up with the resurrected in the rapture of the church. When we see him, our time of grief will be over. We notice in Revelation that the words spoken in Heaven are words of celebration and praise! Things look grim when a believer lies on their death bed, but we need to realize that they are about to enter the most profound and exciting moment of celebration they have ever experienced.

---

[1] Psalm 116:15
[2] Matthew 22:23
[3] Genesis 1:31
[4] Genesis 3:22-24
[5] 1 Corinthians 15:51
[6] 1 Thessalonians 4:13
[7] 2 Corinthians 5:6-9
[8] Many Christians disagree about the makeup of the human. I list these four parts because these are mentioned in Scripture, so we should use Scriptural terms. My intent is not to give an exhaustive description of man, but to simply show that there is a separation of the material part and non-material parts.
[9] Romans 12:2
[10] Ephesians 4:23
[11] Hebrews 4:12
[12] 1 Corinthians 14:32
[13] 1 John 4:1
[14] Catechism of the Catholic Church, Second Edition, (Double Day: 1994), 411.
[15] Acts 1:11
[16] Revelation 19:2
[17] Luke 16:23
[18] Revelation 7:9-10

Chapter 2
Decomposition Re-Commissioned
The resurrection of believers

1 Corinthians 2:9-10 says, *"However, as it is written: "No eye has seen, no ear has heard, no mind has conceived what God has prepared for those who love him"— [10]but God has revealed it to us by his Spirit.* How has the Sprit revealed what we will be like? Through the word of God. The Scriptures are filled with little hints about our future nature, location, work and rewards. Paul told Timothy that, "All Scripture is God-breathed and is useful for teaching, rebuking, correcting and training in righteousness…"[1] The Holy Spirit has revealed what God has prepared for us through the inspiration of Scripture.

It is important to note, that there is no place where any Scripture writer gives us an exhaustive description of the resurrection. The epistles are answering particular local church questions, and prophetic writing is following the direction of the vision or word that is being given at the time from God, not a linear outline. As westerners, we like to read descriptions of events and subjects in well ordered, complete, linear outlines. The Scriptures are not given to us in a purely western format and could not likely be accomplished since the Word speaks to every imaginable subject. By the way, this is a good reminder that western culture is not inspired by God, it is not perfect, nor is it necessarily superior. It has more Christian influence than most cultures, but it has plenty of faults too. This is also a good time to note that the Bible teaches us God's truth in the context of history. Therefore, not all information on any subject is exhaustive, but builds upon the previous information to give a complete picture.

The second way that God is revealing what has been prepared for us is through the illumination of Scriptures by the Holy Spirit. In John 16:13, Jesus says, *"But when he, the Spirit of truth, comes, he will guide you into all truth. He will not speak on his own; he will speak only what he hears, and he will tell you what is yet to come."* We usually quote this verse in regard to discipleship and personal help in Bible study and discovery. However, look at the last few words, *"and he will tell you what is yet to come."* The Spirit will not only illuminate the Scriptures, but he will use the framework of the Scriptures to help us reason and realize the things that are coming in the future.

There are many who have abused this in the past. Setting dates for the Lord's return, and prescribing particular world leaders and nations as particular end time characters is folly. But, we can perceive the signs of the times more accurately with the help of the Holy Spirit.

One of the great things that *"God has prepared for those that love him"* on a very personal and individual level is a new body at the resurrection of believers. There are two key passages of Scripture that give us huge amounts of information on this future blessing for the believer. Read 1 Thessalonians 4:13-18.

¹³Brothers, we do not want you to be ignorant about those who fall asleep, or to grieve like the rest of men, who have no hope. ¹⁴We believe that Jesus died and rose again and so we believe that God will bring with Jesus those who have fallen asleep in him. ¹⁵According to the Lord's own word, we tell you that we who are still alive, who are left till the coming of the Lord, will certainly not precede those who have fallen asleep. ¹⁶For the Lord himself will come down from heaven, with a loud command, with the voice of the archangel and with the trumpet call of God, and the dead in Christ will rise first. ¹⁷After that, we who are still alive and are left will be caught up together with them in the clouds to meet the Lord in the air. And so we will be with the Lord forever. ¹⁸Therefore encourage each other with these words.

Now read 1 Corinthians 15:22-23 and 35-57.

²²For as in Adam all die, so in Christ all will be made alive. ²³But each in his own turn: Christ, the firstfruits; then, when he comes, those who belong to him…

³⁵But someone may ask, "How are the dead raised? With what kind of body will they come?" ³⁶How foolish! What you sow does not come to life unless it dies. ³⁷When you sow, you do not plant the body that will be, but just a seed, perhaps of wheat or of something else. ³⁸But God gives it a body as he has determined, and to each kind of seed he gives its own body. ³⁹All flesh is not the same: Men have one kind of flesh, animals have another, birds another and fish another. ⁴⁰There are also heavenly bodies and there are earthly bodies; but the splendor of the heavenly bodies is one kind, and the splendor of the earthly bodies is another. ⁴¹The sun has one kind of splendor, the moon another and the stars another; and star differs from star in splendor.

⁴²So will it be with the resurrection of the dead. The body that is sown is perishable, it is raised imperishable; ⁴³it is sown in dishonor, it is raised in glory; it is sown in weakness, it is raised in power; ⁴⁴it is sown a natural body, it is raised a spiritual body.

If there is a natural body, there is also a spiritual body. ⁴⁵So it is written: "The first man Adam became a living being"; the last Adam, a life-giving spirit. ⁴⁶The spiritual did not come first, but the natural, and after that the spiritual. ⁴⁷The first man was of the dust of the earth, the second man from heaven. ⁴⁸As was the earthly man, so are those who are of the earth; and as is the man from heaven, so also are those who are of heaven. ⁴⁹And just as we have borne the likeness of the earthly man, so shall we bear the likeness of the man from heaven.

⁵⁰I declare to you, brothers, that flesh and blood cannot inherit the kingdom of God, nor does the perishable inherit the imperishable. ⁵¹Listen, I tell you a mystery: We will not all sleep, but we will all be changed— ⁵²in a flash, in the twinkling of an eye, at the last trumpet. For the trumpet will sound, the dead will be raised imperishable, and we will be changed. ⁵³For the perishable must clothe itself with the imperishable, and the mortal with immortality. ⁵⁴When the perishable has been clothed with the imperishable, and the mortal with immortality, then the saying that is written will come true: "Death has been swallowed up in victory."

⁵⁵"Where, O death, is your victory?

Where, O death, is your sting?" ⁵⁶The sting of death is sin, and the power of sin is the law. ⁵⁷But thanks be to God! He gives us the victory through our Lord Jesus Christ.

I know those are long passages of Scripture to have in a book. If you have never read these Scriptures, you need to read them for the first time. I remember reading these passages for the first time as a senior in high school. I had attended church all my life, but I had never been taught about the resurrection of the believer. I knew the phrase from the Apostle's Creed that I had to memorize in a confirmation class, "we believe in the resurrection of the dead." But I had no idea that it referred to my resurrection! It is a good exercise to read these passages again before we enter into this conversation. Go back and read them again if they are new to you to make sure you are familiar with them. Now, let's get into the meat of this discussion and find out what God has prepared for us physically in eternity.

When Will We Rise?

You may have already realized that this book is following a chronological path through the future events of prophecy if you are a student of Bible prophecy. So, it is important to notice that the next event in prophetic history is the resurrection of believers. 1 Thessalonians 4:16b-17a says, *"and the dead in Christ will rise first. ¹⁷After that, we who are still alive and are left will be caught up together with them in the clouds to meet the Lord in the air."* Paul is talking about a future event in 1 Thessalonians, but in it he lists the various parts of the event in their order. I might invite you to my birthday party, one event. And you might ask what we will be doing. Then I would give you some details about the parts of the event: we will eat cake, open gifts, and watch a movie. This is what Paul is doing here in 1 Thessalonians. The particular events happen so close together and so quickly, that in reality, all the events take place in a flash. Like the party, Jesus is coming again. When he comes, the details are: the trump will sound, the dead will rise, living Christians will be caught up, and we will all be with the Lord forever.

1 Corinthians 15:23 and 52 says there is an order to the various resurrections in the Bible, *"²³But each in his own turn: Christ, the first fruits; then, when he comes, those who belong to him…⁵²in a flash, in the twinkling of an eye, at the last trumpet. For the trumpet will sound, the dead will be raised imperishable, and we will be changed."* In both 1 Thessalonians and 1 Corinthians, Paul tells us that when we rise from the dead, we will receive our new body.

Paul indicates that it will occur at *"the coming of the Lord."*[2] Paul also indicates that Jesus *"will come like a thief in the night."*[3] Jesus said that *"the Son of Man will come at an hour when you do not expect him."*[4] When Jesus returns, his return is unexpected, and in some ways unseen. In the parable of the ten virgins in Matthew chapter 10, the five foolish virgins have missed the groom coming for the bride and they don't even realize that they missed his appearing! Some people find this hard to reconcile with the second coming of Christ to earth in Revelation 19:11 and following. In his second coming to the earth, he comes as *"KING OF KINGS AND LORD OF LORDS"*[5] and *"every eye will see him."*[6] So, how can he come like a thief and like a king? The answer is in the end of 1

Thessalonians chapter four that you just read. There, Paul tells us about the dead rising and the church being caught up (*rapture*) together with the resurrected dead in the clouds with the Lord. That is not the second coming of Jesus to earth. At Jesus' second coming to earth, he will not visit in the air, but will come through the clouds (very visibly to all on earth) and will again set foot on earth.

So, the point regarding timing is that we will receive our new bodies when Jesus returns, not to earth, but in the air, for the resurrected church. This is like I mentioned earlier about being invited to a party. Jesus' returning for the church is the party, or the event. Now let's look at the particular parts of that future event.

Paul says that the dead in Christ will rise first and then the believers who are alive at that time will be caught up with them. There are two parts at the event. The first part is the resurrection of the believers that have already died. The second part is the catching away of the Church that is alive. Either way, the dead in Christ we discussed in chapter one who are experiencing the separation and those of the Church who have not experienced physical death, all Christians will take part in this event that is the return of Christ for the Church.

What Will We Be Like?

The first guiding truth to understanding what we will be like is in 1 Corinthians 15:42-44. The body that we will have will be different from the one we have now, but it will also be the same. Think about verse 42, *"The body that is sown is perishable, it is raised imperishable."* The body that is sown is the body that is raised. But that body is changed. Paul describes that the perishable body is made imperishable, it will not die. The body sown in dishonor is raised in glory. I don't think that *"dishonor"* refers to sex as a dishonorable form of procreation as some may think. Some people think that the rules regarding sex in the Bible mean that all sex is evil, but allowed in marriage to produce children. Sex was the format for filling the earth before sin in Genesis chapter two. Therefore, we can not think of sex as a dishonorable human function within God's design. *"Sown in dishonor"* refers to being created in a sinful world. Since sin entered the world, our bodies are not the imperishable pure things that God created them to be. It is sown in weakness and raised in power. Our bodies will be raised by the power of the Lord. There will be aspects of strength and empowerment in our resurrected bodies that we do not currently have. Finally, the body that is raised is a spiritual body. It will have some spiritual aspect that our current bodies do not have. Perhaps it may be spiritual perception.

The second guiding truth is in 1 Corinthians 15:49 which says, *And just as we have borne the likeness of the earthly man, so shall we bear the likeness of the man from heaven.* Another scripture that says the same thing is 1 John 3:1-3.

> *[1] How great is the love the Father has lavished on us, that we should be called children of God! And that is what we are! The reason the world does not know us is that it did not know him. [2] Dear friends, now we are children of God, and what we will be has not yet been made known. But we know that when he appears, we shall be like him, for we shall see him as he is. [3] Everyone who has this hope in him purifies himself, just as he is pure.*

When Jesus appears for the church we will be changed and *"be like him."* We will never become God, but we will be like Jesus in his resurrected human properties. So, let's look at what we know about him that will tell us what we will be like through the power of God.

The main characteristic of Jesus' resurrected body is that it was his physical body. In Luke 24:39, Jesus challenged the disciples to touch him and see that he really rose from the dead. *Look at my hands and my feet. It is I myself! Touch me and see; a ghost does not have flesh and bones, as you see I have."* In Luke 24:30-32, Jesus walked with two men on the road to Emmaus and appeared to them completely normal, and human. Luke records the end of their journey,

> *When he was at the table with them, he took bread, gave thanks, broke it and began to give it to them. ³¹Then their eyes were opened and they recognized him, and he disappeared from their sight. ³²They asked each other, "Were not our hearts burning within us while he talked with us on the road and opened the Scriptures to us?"*

The men he had walked with that day did not realize any physical difference in Jesus' body. They thought they were walking with a normal man. So, the first note about being like Jesus is that we will have physical resurrected bodies. We will not be ghosts.

The second thing to note about being like Jesus is that his resurrected body was a spiritual body that allowed him some unusual capabilities. John 20:19 records the first appearance of Jesus to his disciples, *On the evening of that first day of the week, when the disciples were together, with the doors locked for fear of the Jews, Jesus came and stood among them and said, "Peace be with you!"* Then, later in verse 26, the second appearance is recorded, *A week later his disciples were in the house again, and Thomas was with them. Though the doors were locked, Jesus came and stood among them and said, "Peace be with you!"* In both instances, Jesus appeared unnaturally in a room with locked doors. Obviously, the inclusion of the locked doors data is to indicate that Jesus appeared, or entered the room, in a manner not like other people who walked through the door. One of the elements of the spiritual body may be the ability to move about differently than we currently do.

Jesus appeared in various places between the Easter morning resurrection and ascension. In the final state of the New Heavens and the New Earth, the subject of chapter seven, it appears that we will be able to travel from heaven to earth. If we are like him not only in character, but in physical resurrected properties, we will have the ability to move about differently. We don't fully understand all that means, or what prerogative the Lord will grant us in that ability. We obviously don't understand the mechanics. But, it seems that we will have extended abilities, not for our own glory or thrills, but for the glory of Jesus Christ.

Here is an interesting thought. We always think of Isaiah 40:31 as a verse about God granting us some sort of spiritual almost mystical strength when we wait upon the Lord. "*...but those who hope in the LORD will renew their strength. They will soar on wings like eagles; they will run and not grow weary, they will walk and not be faint.*" But what if the ultimate fulfillment of that is not only mystical and spiritual, but practical? What if we, who have waited upon the Lord, and have hoped in him, will soar in movements that we currently have no way of understanding? Are we waiting for the Lord's return? Is not the doctrine of the Rapture and the Resurrection also referred to by many as The Blessed Hope?

"…*those who hope in the Lord…will soar…will run…will walk and not be faint.*"

One of the most blessed rewards of eternity will be our glorified, resurrected bodies.

The great thing about this point in time for believers is that they will be totally saved. The work will be accomplished for us. The separation of the body and the soul will be past and the body will join the mind, spirit, and soul in being totally renewed; totally saved body, soul, mind and spirit. 1 Corinthians 2:9-10 says,

> [9]*However, as it is written:*
> *"No eye has seen,*
>   *no ear has heard,*
> *no mind has conceived*
>   *what God has prepared for those who love him"*— [10]*but God has revealed it to us by his Spirit.*

---

[1] 1 Timothy 3:16
[2] 1 Thessalonians 4:15
[3] 1 Thessalonians 5:2
[4] Matthew 24:44
[5] Revelation 19:16
[6] Revelation 1:7

Chapter 3
Going, Going, Gone!
The Rapture of the Church

Have you ever wanted to be a secret agent? Are you drawn by the espionage intrigue, action, danger, and excitement? In a way, you are! We are aliens and strangers in this world. Our citizenship is elsewhere. And we have a mission to accomplish before we go home, to bring as many friends and relatives with us as possible. Try thinking of yourself as a secret agent who is commissioned to turn the enemies' troops to our side.

Really, you are simply following Jesus' example. Two thousand years ago, Jesus very secretly snuck into our world as a little baby. He came as the King of Kings, the answer to every Old Testament prophecy, and to be the only sacrifice for every sin committed in the entire history of the world. Jesus came to start an institution that would claim 2.2 billion followers by 2,000 A.D., to change the Roman Empire in 300 years, and to become the greatest known figure in history! *But, he came secretly.*

Think about the people who knew, like a socially rejected couple on an awkward trip. They were poor and unknown. Three astronomers, a handful of shepherds, one old lady and one old man ministering at a worship center in Jerusalem soon to be demolished. Considering his mission and his impact, Jesus came very secretly.

He has done many unseen and unpublished miracles since his first advent. Billions have been re-born. He has provided food, not for a few thousand, but for millions of his followers. He has calmed innumerable storms. He has made the lame walk, cancers disappear, and healed more than could be recorded. He has transmitted his wisdom through the Holy Sprit to millions in his army of secret agents. But most of these are sadly unpublished, unnoticed, sometimes unappreciated, and even unaccepted.

He has been working quietly and powerfully since his first advent. His followers have tried to publish his works, but all publications are always a few steps behind him. He does his secret work and we find out a moment later. Then we must accept by faith that it really was him that did the work! He moves so secretly that his skeptics pounce on the questions left unanswered.

So, what is the next big secret move of God? It is Jesus returning for his secret agents. He will enter the earth's atmosphere and will raise the physical bodies of all who have served him. Then he will cause all those serving him to be changed in an instant and they will meet him in the air. The world will certainly have questions about the loss of millions of people, but then again, it will be done in secret, unpublished, unannounced, and to know what really happened, those left behind will have to accept the truth by faith. But since they did not accept the truth of his work before, they will not accept it now. Furthermore, there will be a lie that they will be given that will suit their pleasures better, and they will reject the truth of his catching away of his secret agents. 2 Thessalonians 2:11 says that this lie will be a *"strong delusion."* If the Church is no longer around to counter Satan's lies, people will believe them.

Then, after seven years of God working in more drastic ways on earth to turn the hearts of those left behind, Jesus will break out of his secret agent mode and will come again to earth as a king with a giant army with him. They will come so that the entire world will see them. He and his army will set up an earthly kingdom which Jesus will rule for 1,000 years. If you believe that Jesus fulfilled the Scriptures in his first advent, just wait till he fulfills the promises of Scripture for his second advent and for the rescue mission of the saints at the rapture of the church.

What can I tell you about the day when Jesus will catch us away to be with him? That is the subject of this chapter. Let's look at some scriptures. In chapter two I had you read 1 Thessalonians 4:13-18 and 1 Corinthians 15. It may be handy for you to bookmark those passages in your Bible and keep it handy while you read.

Jesus is Coming Soon.

One of the key points of the message of the gospel in the first century church was this point, Jesus is coming soon. From the very start of New

Testament preaching on the Day of Pentecost in Acts two, the focus on the return of Christ has been one of the points of effectively conveying the gospel. In Acts chapter two, Peter pointed his listeners to a prophetic passage from Joel 2:28-32.

> *28 "And afterward,*
> *I will pour out my Spirit on all people.*
> *Your sons and daughters will prophesy,*
> *your old men will dream dreams,*
> *your young men will see visions.*
> *29 Even on my servants, both men and women,*
> *I will pour out my Spirit in those days.*
> *30 I will show wonders in the heavens*
> *and on the earth,*
> *blood and fire and billows of smoke.*
> *31 The sun will be turned to darkness*
> *and the moon to blood*
> *before the coming of the great and dreadful day of the LORD.*
> *32 And everyone who calls*
> *on the name of the LORD will be saved;*
> *for on Mount Zion and in Jerusalem*
> *there will be deliverance,*
> *as the LORD has said,*
> *among the survivors*
> *whom the LORD calls.*

Using this passage at that time painted a picture, a timeline for the listeners on the Day of Pentecost. The picture tells them, "You are living in the last days." Peter let them know that time was short! The days were numbered. God is pouring out his Spirit in these last days just before *"the great and dreadful day of the Lord."*

Furthermore, we also have the words of Jesus to John in Revelation. *"I am coming soon. Hold on to what you have, so that no one will take your crown."* "Behold, I am coming soon! My reward is with me, and I will give to everyone according to what he has *done."²* Jesus intends for Christians to share the good news of the gospel with an ending that is exciting, not scary. It can be scary, if a person is not right with God. But the message is good news from start to finish. The last bit of good news is that Jesus is coming again. Too often we use his coming as this horrible scare tactic. Jesus did that in many of his parables, so it is not unbiblical, but Jesus coming again was not bad news to the first disciples. It was the final stroke of good news in the gospel (good news) message.

Obviously, there are many who have discarded this message because it has been two thousand years. Some discard the message by avoiding the subject and never preaching on it. "Oh, we can't preach like that. A visitor might be offended or think that our message is too radical and not come again to our church!" I say that people need to hear the whole gospel message and if we present Jesus' return as good news, they will get excited about his return too! Others discard the message that Jesus is coming soon by changing their doctrine and their views on the Biblical narrative. They say, "Since it has been so long, the events in the Bible prophecy can not be literal events, but are imagery, pictures of truth about our world."

Remember 2 Peter 3:8-9,

> "*⁸But do not forget this one thing, dear friends: With the Lord a day is like a thousand years, and a thousand years are like a day. ⁹The Lord is not slow in keeping his promise, as some understand slowness. He is patient with you, not wanting anyone to perish, but everyone to come to repentance.*"

This comparison of a day to 1,000 years is not intended to be a mathematical formula, but a description of how God views time. Waiting a few thousand years is not a long time to Jesus. He was present at the creation of the world! He waited far longer to arrive the first time. He is still coming soon.

Jesus is Coming Unexpectedly.

If we believe that Jesus is coming soon, then how can his appearance be unexpected? The answer is, though we are told he is coming soon, we are not told when he is coming. *"No one knows about that day or hour, not even the angels in heaven, nor the Son, but only the Father."*[3] The Bible says that when Jesus returns it will be like it was in the days before the flood. People were going about their business like nothing strange was about to happen.[4] Then, as if without warning, the flood hit. Interestingly, it was with warning. Noah had been preaching about the flood and building this crazy boat, hundreds of miles from water for one hundred and twenty years! Maybe everyone got used to watching Noah build the boat for over a century. This may be the same with us today. We preach that Jesus is coming soon yet the skeptics say you have been preaching that for two thousand years. You are obviously wrong. But, bit by bit, we are building the Church, and one day those who have found refuge in it will be saved and those left outside will face the destruction of the tribulation. Yes, a lot like Noah's days!

Jesus gives a great warning to us about his unexpected return. *"Be careful, or your hearts will be weighed down with dissipation, drunkenness and the anxieties of life, and that day will close on you unexpectedly like a trap."*[5] I have always been curious about the word *"dissipation."* Men, have you ever burned something in the kitchen?

Even something as simple as a fried egg can be a fire hazard with some of us guys. As a young teen I started a cooking project with oil in a pan and then went to watch TV while it heated up. Of course I forgot about it. A few moments later, smoke was filling the living room and I ran to the kitchen to find flames shooting up the cabinets to the ceiling. The lasting effects of my culinary adventure were with that house till my parents moved out of it twenty years later. However, there was something that stuck in my mind that was not a lasting effect on my parents' kitchen. That was the smoke. Smoke dissipates. I will never forget the height of the flames and the thickness of the smoke in that room. But, the flames died down and the smoke dissipated.

How many of us will never forget the flame of the Spirit in our hearts when we were first forgiven by God. How many of us will never forget the tears of sorrow for our sins and tears of joy for our forgiveness when we started following Jesus. We never forget those amazing experiences. But we allow the fire to die down and the smoke to dissipate. Jesus told us what the **cause** of dissipation would be, *"...hearts weighed down with dissipation, drunkenness and the anxieties of life..."* Are we going to be unaware on the day Jesus comes because we have let the fire for our first love die out? Are we going to be unaware because of sins of omission? Sin's of omission are not the things we consciously do wrong, but the things we forget or choose not to do. Are we going to be unaware because of all the other "gods" of this life that have become more important than Jesus? One reason to stay close to Christ and walk daily with him is to keep from being weighed down with dissipation. Stay sharp in the Lord and expectant of his return.

Jesus told us in several parables like the parable of the vineyard workers, the ten virgins, the wheat and the tares, and the talents that he would be returning unannounced, unexpectedly. The Bible actually says that most of the world will be surprised at the day of the Lord. Even as I write these words on my computer I realize that I have not been expecting his coming during my study time! Obviously, those who reject Christ will be unaware, but most of those who claim to follow Christ will not be thinking, "Jesus might come today." Faithful Christians may be caught unaware, but they will be ready.

Jesus is Coming in a Flash!

My kids loved *The Incredibles*, the movie about the superhero family. My boys liked Flash the most. He moved so fast he was unseen, like a bullet from a gun. The kids watched the movie in quiet attention. Then after the movie, they went crazy in the house attempting to be incredible! The post-movie situations became so wild that we had to shelf the DVD for awhile. In 1 Corinthians 15:51-52, Paul tells us a hint of how fast Jesus will return for the church.

> *"Listen, I tell you a mystery: We will not all sleep, but we will all be changed— in a flash, in the twinkling of an eye, at the last trumpet. For the trumpet will sound, the dead will be raised imperishable, and we will be changed."*

All the searching I have done indicates that the human eye blinks about ten times per minute. A blink takes about 300 to 400 milliseconds, that is, three tenths to four tenths of a second. We blink so fast that we don't even realize we do it that often. Jesus will return for the church in a flash, or in the twinkling of an eye, in a blink. There will be no time to prepare, no time to decide to follow Christ. It will happen so fast that those who are unprepared, but understand the situation that just occurred, will have no time to react.

I have friends who do emergency response, medical missionary work. They live differently from other people. They bought a condo, keep a huge savings account, keep unusual medications in their cabinet, are vaccinated for everything, and keep a special bank account that can be accessed quickly and easily. Why do they live like this? To be ready at a moment's notice. The pay off has been opportunities to minister after earthquakes, tsunamis and hurricanes all over the world. As Christians, we ought to live a bit differently; we live for the Lord, not for this life. Why? Because, he might return any moment. The instruction of the Bible is to live ready for Jesus' coming.

Jesus is Coming in the Air.

At first glance, this statement, coming in the air, seems really crazy. Why is Jesus coming in the air? Keep in mind that there are two aspects of Jesus' coming again. The first aspect is what is commonly called the rapture of the church or Christ's return for the church in the air. The second aspect is called the "second coming" when he arrives on the earth. (By the way, the "first coming" of Jesus to earth, advent, was when Christ came to the earth as a babe in a manger.) Jesus coming in the air, and his second coming to earth, are two completely separate events. The rapture of the church is described in I

Thessalonians 4:17. At that time Christ will not come completely to earth. He will meet us in the air to quickly accomplish what he came for at that time. There are events that must then take place before his "second coming". This will be covered in greater detail in a later chapter.

What do I mean when I say, coming in the air? 1 Thessalonians 4:17 says, *"After that, we who are still alive and are left will be caught up together with them in the clouds to meet the Lord in the air."* When Jesus comes for the Church he will come close to the earth and the church, those resurrected and those caught away, will meet him in the air. He will not come to earth until we return with him in his second coming (this is the subject of a later chapter). There are two events related to Jesus coming again. The first is his return for the Church (rapture and resurrection), and the second is, his return to earth (the second coming). When the term second coming is used it means his second coming to the earth. When the term rapture is used it has to do with the catching away of the church.

Jesus is Coming to Save Us From Wrath.

As an Assembly of God minister, I sign a document each December stating that I will continue to adhere to and preach the 16 fundamental truths of our fellowship of ministers. One of those fundamental truths is called *The Blessed Hope*. I could not understand why it was called *"The Blessed Hope"* for a long time. I thought it was just about being with Jesus, and that is still the primary blessing of heaven. Then I learned it was also about the resurrection of our bodies, and I do hope for the blessing of the resurrection of my body. But there is another reason that this doctrine of the rapture is a blessed hope. 1 Thessalonians 1:9b-10 says, *"They tell how you turned to God from idols to serve the living and true God, ¹⁰and to wait for his Son from heaven, whom he raised from the dead— Jesus, who rescues us from the coming wrath."* Our hope is not only the blessing of the Lord's presence and a new body, there is our hope of being spared (saved) from the wrath of God. The horrible things that happen to the earth in Revelation are the events of what is called the tribulation. Consider these three other factors in our being saved from the wrath that is coming.

First, it is important to understand the purpose of God's wrath. This is wrath with a purpose, not a mad or bitter revenge. From the very beginning of the Bible, God's punitive actions have been motivated by a desire to redeem, not an angry desire to retaliate. In Genesis 3:17, Adam and Eve were banished from the garden, not in anger, but with logic and love. God did not want mankind to have access to the Tree of Life in a sinful state and thus live forever full of sin, shame, wrong thinking and living. The motive for banishment was to save Adam, Eve, and all their future children. In the same way, the wrath of the last days described in Revelation is not retaliatory, but redemptive. God is trying to get the attention of the lost. The saved have already placed their attention upon the Lord, so they are free from wrath.

Second, this is the last seven years decreed for God's people, Israel, to be saved. Daniel foretold of 70 sets of seven years for God to work on the hearts of Israel in Daniel 9:24.

"Seventy 'sevens' are decreed for your people and your holy city to finish transgression, to put an end to sin, to atone for wickedness, to bring in everlasting righteousness, to seal up vision and prophecy and to anoint the most holy.

The focus of this time is not on the Gentiles, but the descendants of Abraham. How amazing is the Bible? This amazing; Daniel received a vision that indicated that the king of Persia would give a command to rebuild the temple in Jerusalem. At the moment of that command, 70 sets of seven years would begin to tick off in history. Four hundred and eighty three years later (7 x 69 = 483), Jesus dies on the cross, leaving one set of 7 yet to be completed. That one set will be completed in the 7 years of tribulation in the book of Revelation. There is far more amazing detail about this vision of Daniel and the accuracy of Scripture when measured against the historical account. However, the focus here is simply to say that Christ's wrath has a purpose. New Testament saints do not fit the requirements of those who deserve wrath and are saved from the wrath that is coming. The Jews are the focus in Revelation chapters 7 and 12. Most of the Old Testament is focused on God's promises to the Jews and his plan to use them to bless the world. God is still keeping his promise to them and will forever!

Third, and finally, the church must be removed so that the spirit of the antichrist, who is in the world now, will be free to do as he wishes. 1 John 4:1-3 tells us that the spirit of the antichrist is in the world now, *"but every spirit that does not acknowledge Jesus is not from God. This is the spirit of the antichrist, which you have heard is coming and even now is already in the world."* Though the spirit of antichrist is in the world, it is being held back from accomplishing its real satanic desires.

"And now you know what is holding him back, so that he may be revealed at the proper time. For the secret power of lawlessness is already at work; but the one who now holds it back will continue to do so till he is taken out of the way."[6] It is an amazing thought to realize the power of the Church on earth to influence the world for godliness. The Church, empowered by the Spirit and directed by Christ, is holding back the powers of Satan that wish to control this world. The next time Satan tries to tell you that the Church does not really matter in our culture today, remember that the church is holding the spirit of antichrist in check right now!

Consider all the promises God kept for his Son to come to earth the first time. Think about all the amazing details that he accomplished to have him arrive at just the right time and place. Jesus was born in Bethlehem, just as the prophet foretold[7], but just barely! Had he been born a few hours earlier, who knows where his birth would have occurred. Consider what Jesus did for you on the cross. Consider how secretly Jesus arrived the first time and how unannounced he will come again. Realize that God is able to make all the situations perfect for Jesus to come again for you. Make your decision right now to accept him and be ready for his return for the Church. You do not want to miss the first of all the end time events, the rapture of the Church.

---

[1] Revelation 3:11
[2] Revelation 22:12
[3] Mark 13:32
[4] Luke 17:26-29
[5] Luke 21:34
[6] 1 Thessalonians 2:6-7
[7] Micah 5:2

Chapter 4
Celebrate! Celebrate!
The Wedding Supper

A Biblical researcher I worked with in seminary told me the following joke. A Roman Catholic monk of the ninth century died in his monastery in Europe. He had spent his life researching the oldest manuscripts of the Bible trying to learn what he could from those early texts, wishing he could read the original manuscripts of Paul and the Apostles.

Arriving in heaven, Saint Peter said to him, "What would you like to do first?" The monk said, "I want to read the original texts!" Peter took him to the library and showed him the various scrolls and letters. He left him in the quiet library for hours.

Hours later, Saint Peter returned to hear the man tearing the library apart violently and yelling. Saint Peter entered the room and yelled for the monk to stop. Then he grabbed the monk and said, "What is wrong with you man!" The monk replied emphatically, "The original text says, 'celebrate, celebrate!'"

Seriously, there are many places in the Scripture where we are instructed to celebrate and rejoice. Philippians 4:4 says, *"Rejoice in the Lord always. I will say it again: Rejoice!"* There are examples of God's people celebrating and rejoicing as in Exodus 15:21.

> *Miriam sang to them:*
> *"Sing to the LORD,*
> *for he is highly exalted.*
> *The horse and its rider*
> *he has hurled into the sea."*

God did not make you to be bored and bothered by religion. He made us to celebrate and rejoice in a relationship with him. That is why we believe in spontaneous worship, passionate, contemporary, and zealous worship.

However, the greatest celebration is coming. The greatest time of rejoicing is not here and now, but in the future. The book of Revelation lines out for us chronologically all the events of the last days from the days between the church age (chapters 1-3) and the creation of the New Heavens and the New Earth (chapter 21 and 22).

A Wedding Story

In Revelation 19, the writer, John, is swept up and out of the earthly realm that has been plagued by the wrath of God and the spirit of the Antichrist for seven years. We are swept up into heaven where we find the saints (including you and me) doing what you would expect after the rapture, resurrection, and the fulfillment of God's promises. CELEBRATING!!! That celebration is called *"the wedding supper of the Lamb."*

So, what is the wedding supper of the Lamb? For that matter, what is a wedding supper? To really understand this title that is given to the celebration in heaven we need to understand how the term related to a first century wedding. Second, we need to understand the imagery of a wedding that is evident all through the New Testament to describe the relationship of Jesus to his Church. Both of these goals can be reached by researching the first century Jewish wedding custom and celebration. Let me tell you a wedding story.

There were four major parts to a first century Jewish wedding[1]. First, a marriage contract was consummated between the parents of the bride and the bridegroom, with the parents of the bride paying a dowry to the bridegroom or his parents. This was called the betrothal period. Today it is called the engagement. This is the time in which Mary was found to be with child in the Christmas story.[2] This period usually lasted at least one year, but could last longer depending on the age of the couple.

While serving as an Associate Pastor in Jefferson City, Missouri, I became friends with several couples from India. As my wife and I got to know these friends, we found out quickly that their marriages had been arranged. We had never met anyone like this. I asked one of these friends how long he knew his wife before they were married. He had only met her one time, two months before they were married! My wife and I were baffled at the prospect of hardly knowing a person before being married to them. We learned from that experience that people don't "fall in love." People fall in holes, fall off ladders and fall over obstacles. People choose to love. Choose to love your husband or your wife.

It is amazing that God chose to use this type of marriage to illustrate his relationship to us. When we think of engagement today, we think of the romance, the adventure and the stress of dating and finding the "right one." But, the illustration in Scripture of the Church's betrothal to Christ is a picture of the Father in Heaven arranging a relationship between us (the bride) and his Son Jesus. We did not choose Jesus, nor did we find him on our own power. God the father arranged the relationship for us. He determined when we should live,[3] he sent his son for us, and he drew our interests toward Jesus. We have a part in responding to God, but if he had not arranged our relationship to Christ, we would have been powerless to respond.

The second step in the first century Jewish wedding usually occurred a year later. The groom would take that year to build a house for the bride. In John 14:1-3, Jesus is talking to the disciples just before he was betrayed. It was his last chance to give instruction to them before his death and resurrection. In that setting he said,

> "Do not let your hearts be troubled. Trust in God; trust also in me. In my Father's house are many rooms; if it were not so, I would have told you. I am going there to prepare a place for you. And if I go and prepare a place for you, I will come back and take you to be with me that you also may be where I am.

Jesus was explaining that he would have to leave for a while, but in that absence he would be preparing a place for us in his Father's house. That is the exact picture of a wedding in that day. Jesus, the groom, is engaged to us. He is preparing a room or addition to his Father's house for you and me. Soon, Jesus will begin the next step in his marriage to the Church.

The third step began at the completion of the house or room addition. The bridegroom would gather his friends and go to the bride's house at midnight to get her. The bride would know this was going to take place. The image was of him stealing her, but the date was well known. The bride would be ready with her friends, and they would join the late night parade that would end at the bridegroom's home. This was the common picture Jesus used in the parable of the virgins in Matthew 25:1-13. In the wedding story between the Church and Jesus Christ, this will occur at the rapture of the Church. The groom will arrive at the bride's door to steal her away to the place he has prepared for her.

The fourth step was the wedding supper itself, which might go on for days. This kind of wedding celebration is found in John 2:1-2. Jesus was invited to a wedding celebration in Cana. The celebration lasted several days resulting in the party running out of wine. There were likely scores of guests and the amount of wine Jesus created does not indicate a drunken party, but the length of the party and the huge number of family and guests. The wedding supper of the Lamb is simply the end of the engagement period and the uniting of the bride to the groom. The series of events in a first century Jewish wedding serve as an illustration of the events that have and will transpire between the church (the bride) and Jesus Christ (the groom).

Now you can see why Paul uses the Church/Christ relationship to illustrate the Christian marriage relationship in Ephesians 5:22-25. "Husbands love your wives as Christ loves the church..." It is an illustrative relationship that Jesus used in the gospels and in Revelation. Jesus used a common cultural practice of the day to illustrate his relationship to us and to illustrate the progression of events in the prophetic history/future of the church.

So, will all humanity attend the wedding supper of the Lamb? The answer is no. In the parable of the ten virgins in Matthews 25:1-13, five of the virgins are left out of the celebration. Everyone is invited, but not everyone is prepared when the groom arrives to steal the bride away. Who will be there? The wedding feast will be attended by all the Old Testament saints, New Testament believers, (resurrected and raptured) and those being saved out of the tribulation.[4] The Old Testament saints who loved the Lord and passed away trusting in God's promise of the savior will be a part of the resurrection of believers. The New Testament saints who loved the Lord and passed away trusting in God's accomplished work through Jesus Christ will also be present. These two groups will be involved in the celebration for its entire seven year period. Part of the time may be taken up by the giving of rewards at the judgment seat of Christ, which will be a celebration of its own. It is like the bride opening gifts at a wedding celebration! Finally, there will be some who join the celebration mid-stream. There will be some who are saved through faith in Jesus during the tribulation and they will be joining the celebration that is already in progress.

Now, let's look at the Scriptures in Revelation 19:1-10 where we get the term, *"wedding supper of the lamb."*

¹*After this I heard what sounded like the roar of a great multitude in heaven shouting:*
"Hallelujah!
Salvation and glory and power belong to our God,
²for true and just are his judgments.
He has condemned the great prostitute
who corrupted the earth by her adulteries.
He has avenged on her the blood of his servants." ³And again they shouted:
"Hallelujah!
The smoke from her goes up for ever and ever."
⁴The twenty-four elders and the four living creatures fell down and worshiped God, who was seated on the throne. And they cried:
"Amen, Hallelujah!"
⁵Then a voice came from the throne, saying:
"Praise our God,
all you his servants,
you who fear him,
both small and great!"
⁶Then I heard what sounded like a great multitude, like the roar of rushing waters and like loud peals of thunder, shouting:
"Hallelujah!
For our Lord God Almighty reigns.
⁷Let us rejoice and be glad
and give him glory!
For the wedding of the Lamb has come,
and his bride has made herself ready.
⁸Fine linen, bright and clean,
was given her to wear." (Fine linen stands for the righteous acts of the saints.)
⁹Then the angel said to me, "Write: 'Blessed are those who are invited to the wedding supper of the Lamb!'" And he added, "These are the true words of God."
¹⁰At this I fell at his feet to worship him. But he said to me, "Do not do it! I am a fellow servant with you and with your brothers who hold to the testimony of Jesus. Worship God! For the testimony of Jesus is the spirit of prophecy."

Looking at this descriptive passage of Scripture, we can determine what we will be doing during the wedding supper of the lamb. The celebration is marked by three components.

Shouts of Adoration

"After this I heard what sounded like the roar of a great multitude in heaven shouting:
"Hallelujah!"

We the saints will be worshiping God and praising him at this celebration. Not quietly, but with loud cries of praise. The word Hallelujah is shouted four times. I say shouted because it has an exclamation point every time! I know this may sound strange, but I encourage you to stop reading right now and shout Hallelujah four times.

Often, visitors to the church I pastor wonder why we praise loudly. People wonder why our services are not the stayed liturgies of human recitation and religion. It is because we have such a great future! We see in the scriptures examples of quiet prayer and communication to God. But even when *"Hannah was praying in her heart"*[5] it was so passionate and spontaneous that Eli, the priest, thought she was drunk! We have taken the example of Hannah praying in her heart and made it a proof text for satisfaction with halfhearted, impassionate, quiet praying.

The weight of Scripture points to verbal communication with God.[6] Christians need to learn to pray out loud and praise out loud. Pastors expect their church members to share their faith (verbal), but they have not even taught them to pray their own spontaneous prayers and offer their own spontaneous words of praise. How can we expect Christians to feel prepared to share their faith spontaneously at work or in public when they can't even pray or worship spontaneously in the church? The examples of Scripture show us that communication with God should be verbal and spontaneous, as opposed to praying in our thoughts only and reciting others' prayers only.

The hallmark of real worship is not that it is relevant or contemporary, though one of my core values is relevant and contemporary worship. The real hallmark of heartfelt worship that develops our relationship with Jesus is spontaneous worship. Many churches today use contemporary worship methods calling themselves charismatic or spirit-filled. Though that worship may be spirited, like a pep-rally, it is still a human program and liturgy if it does not allow for the Holy Spirit's direction and spontaneity in the people of God during prayer and worship. The term, "charismatic church" does not have to do with personal charisma. In Biblical terms, it refers to the gifts of the Holy Sprit in the Church. Many churches have a very spirited and contemporary form of liturgy. Everything is programmed from high-tech lighting cues and video components, to the jokes and parts of the service that are intended to make it have the appearance of a casual setting. The leadership of the church is serious and intentional about being casual on the surface, but in reality it is nothing near casual. It is really a highly engineered vainer of hip, cool, relational church.

Spontaneous worship is like a spring that runs over from deep, deep inside us. It is a natural impulse, unconstrained, arising from an internal force. We should be "bursting at the seams". We can hardly imagine being in God's presence having experienced several of the end time prophecies in person! A shout of adoration will surely spring up from inside of us. To suppress it may be impossible!

The marriage supper of the Lamb will be exciting! People shout when they are really excited. Let's free ourselves from the rules that we have placed upon ourselves and our churches. God is a God of order, but he is also a God that evokes an impulsive shout of praise and celebration from the overwhelmed heart of one who has been forgiven, redeemed, and empowered by the Holy Spirit!

Signs of Accomplishment

"He has condemned the great prostitute
  who corrupted the earth by her adulteries.
He has avenged on her the blood of his servants." 3And again they shouted:
"Hallelujah!"

Nothing makes a group of people more pleased than to feel a sense of accomplishment. The saints have seen with their own eyes the fulfillment of many Bible prophecies. The church was raised and raptured. The Seals have been opened. The wrath of God accomplished. The Antichrist revealed. We are in heaven with the Lord, we see him face to face, and our faith is sight. We have seen the prophecies fulfilled!

Imagine what it will be like, when we are looking at Bible prophecy and it is almost all past! History! Historical facts that we have seen with our own resurrected eyes! We almost cannot imagine the feeling of that perspective from our puny vantage point today. But then, it will be magnificent. We can't help but shout Hallelujah again!

Shouts of Agreement

"⁴The twenty-four elders and the four living creatures fell down and worshiped God, who was seated on the throne. And they cried:
  "Amen, Hallelujah!"
⁵Then a voice came from the throne, saying:
  "Praise our God,
    all you his servants,
   you who fear him,
    both small and great!"⁷

Next in the future celebration that John observes, the twenty four elders that surround the throne of God join in the praise. The saints have been worshiping, also there are other creatures in heaven that join in the praise with shouts of agreement. The, *"Amen, Hallelujah!"* is a shout of agreement.

John is taken up to heaven in Revelation 4:4, and shown the throne of God. Surrounding the throne are twenty four thrones with twenty four elders seated on them. It is likely that the twenty four elders are the twelve tribal heads of Israel and the twelve New Testament Apostles. Thus, these individuals are human beings, saints representing the Old and New Testaments. At the Wedding Supper of the Lamb, the participants in praise include all the saints, but the praise of the twenty four elders is singled out and written down by John.

Imagine the excitement of worshiping with the twelve Apostles and the twelve heads of the tribes of Israel. Their praise will be thrilling in the context of heaven. There will be amazing depth of meaning to their praise since we know their stories. To hear Thomas, once a doubter, turned to evangelist who affected the salvations of thousands or millions of Christians in India. When Catholics arrived in India in the 7th century they found Christians who called themselves, "Thomasites." When the Catholics told them they were accountable to the Pope, they said, who's the Pope? We have been serving Jesus without him for six hundred years. I can't wait to hear Thomas' praise. I think about James, the first martyr of the church. I can't wait to hear him praise the Lord. I want to see the look on Peter's face as he praises the Lord. Jesus is called the Lion of the Tribe of Judah. I can't wait to see Judah praising the lion of his tribe. Can you imagine the humility and the depth of praise from Judah, the ancient ancestor of Jesus? I named my son after Benjamin, and I can't wait to meet his namesake. I will join him in praise of our wonderful Messiah, our Savior, our Jesus. Benjamin, the son of Jacob, spent his life looking forward to Jesus while I have spent my life looking back, dependent on Jesus' forgiveness offered through the cross. What an amazing time of worship we will have in heaven!

Next, the shouts of agreement begin to come from an unexpected source! Look at Revelation 19:5.

⁵Then a voice came from the throne, saying:
"Praise our God,
all you his servants,
you who fear him,
both small and great!"

Notice where the next few words of encouragement come from, they come from the throne! God himself joins in the shouts of agreement! I think this is one amazing event. God is moved by the praise of his servants. I watch my kids when they get excited, they can't keep their mouths shut. They shout, yell, whoop, and even jump up and down. God created us in his image. He is described as having perfect and holy emotions that are duplicated in us. God gets angry, sad, happy, and I think he gets excited. The angels get excited and rejoice when a human is saved. I think we have a picture here of God getting excited. Notice that God's words are shouts of agreement! There is an exclamation point after his comment. As God relates to his people, he has the feelings of relationship including celebration and excitement. Because of the liturgical droning of many Christians over the centuries we often tend to have a very liturgical sounding playback mode for Scripture as we read it and meditate on it in our minds. However, I don't think that God says, *"Praise our God, all you his servants, you who fear him, both small and great!"* in a stayed liturgical way. I hear God shouting in excited encouragement and confirmation to his people. He is like a father cheering at his kids' ball game. Did your dad ever embarrass you by getting excited at your game? Your Heavenly Father is excited for you. He is shouting like a soldier who stands victorious on the field of battle with his surviving friends. He is like the general who went into the battle with us, fought the enemy himself, at our side and now we stand together shouting in passionate joy over the victory that we are privileged to enjoy.

Secure Your Answer

To conclude this description of the Wedding Supper of the Lamb, an angel speaks to John, *"Write: 'Blessed are those who are invited to the wedding supper of the Lamb!'"* He added, *"These are the true words of God."* The angel that is showing John what the marriage supper will be like turns to him and instructs him to write down a message. The angel knows that John has access to people who can benefit from what he has seen. It is like he is saying to John, "Do you see this? You have to go back and tell everyone what you just saw! This is how awesome, fun, powerful, and magnificent the celebration will be in heaven. Now go tell everyone! I am an angel, I am not commissioned to tell them, but you are!"

One of the great truths of the New Testament era is that God has put the gospel message in jars of clay. The message is in us, in Christians. God could send angels to share the gospel with people, but he does not do it. He may use angels to point people to other people, but the gospel is always communicated from one person to another. Consider Acts 8:26. An angel appeared to Philip and instructed him to go south to the road that runs to the deserts south of Palestine. He is obedient to the angel and there he meets the Ethiopian Eunuch and shares Jesus with him. It is traditionally believed that Coptic Christians in Ethiopia trace their faith back to this convert (again, it is worth noting that not all Christians trace their roots back to Rome). Think of this amazing truth. Why did God send an angel to Philip? It would have been more convincing to the Ethiopian if he had seen the angel himself. Instead, the Ethiopian was allowed to place his trust in Jesus through the story of Jesus conveyed by a human being who was flawed, and quite normal. This forced the Ethiopian to express faith in God through the message preached. His faith was not in an angel or a vision, but in the message, the good news of Jesus and his story. God will never send an angel or dead saints' spirits to share the gospel with your friends, he has already sent you. Even in the writing of the Scriptures, God's words to us, God primarily used people to proclaim his message.

What did the angel do in this passage of Scripture? He instructed John to invite everyone to attend this wedding supper. God has sent you an RSVP to this party. Will you attend? Secure your answer by confessing your sins and faults. Repent, that is turn away from wicked activities and thoughts. Ask Jesus to forgive you and start following him. When you do, he will bless you with the Holy Spirit to guide you, to share your faith, and to be holy.

---

[1] The information for steps one, three, and four are from *Gotquestions.org*. http://www.gotquestions.org/marriage-supper-Lamb.html (accessed January 2009).
[2] Matthew 1:18 and Luke 2:5
[3] Acts 17:26
[4] These individuals will not likely have resurrected bodies, though they will be in heaven for their confessed faith during their life on earth. Their resurrection will occur at the general resurrection and they will be raised to live forever.
[5] 1 Samuel 1:13
[6] Hebrews 5:7 says that Jesus prayed with loud cries and James 5:16, especially in the King James Version, suggests that fervent prayer is effective.
[7] Revelation 19:4-5

Chapter 5
Riding in the Clouds
The believer's part in the second coming.

I spoke to our youth group recently. I decided to give a really short message and then open the remaining time up to a question and answer session. One of the first questions was about heaven. A sixteen year old girl who had been attending our youth group for about a year asked, "When we get to heaven will we get to fly and will I get a unicorn?" She thought that heaven would really be great if those two wishes could be granted. At first I was a bit stunned. I had never been asked if unicorns were in heaven. But then I thought about Revelation 19:11-21.

In this section of John's revelation of future events, he sees Jesus coming again to earth. Jesus has been absent from the earth since his ascension into heaven recorded in Acts 1:9. He left with a small group of disciples looking on bewildered and confused. He will return so that every eye will see him, confident and powerful. Read Revelation 19:11-21.

"11I saw heaven standing open and there before me was a white horse, whose rider is called Faithful and True. With justice he judges and makes war. 12His eyes are like blazing fire, and on his head are many crowns. He has a name written on him that no one knows but he

himself. *¹³He is dressed in a robe dipped in blood, and his name is the Word of God. ¹⁴The armies of heaven were following him, riding on white horses and dressed in fine linen, white and clean. ¹⁵Out of his mouth comes a sharp sword with which to strike down the nations. "He will rule them with an iron scepter." He treads the winepress of the fury of the wrath of God Almighty. ¹⁶On his robe and on his thigh he has this name written:*
    KING OF KINGS AND LORD OF LORDS.
¹⁷And I saw an angel standing in the sun, who cried in a loud voice to all the birds flying in midair, "Come, gather together for the great supper of God, ¹⁸so that you may eat the flesh of kings, generals, and mighty men, of horses and their riders, and the flesh of all people, free and slave, small and great."
¹⁹Then I saw the beast and the kings of the earth and their armies gathered together to make war against the rider on the horse and his army. ²⁰But the beast was captured, and with him the false prophet who had performed the miraculous signs on his behalf. With these signs he had deluded those who had received the mark of the beast and worshiped his image. The two of them were thrown alive into the fiery lake of burning sulfur. ²¹The rest of them were killed with the sword that came out of the mouth of the rider on the horse, and all the birds gorged themselves on their flesh.

After a few seconds of not knowing what to say, I took this young woman to Revelation 19. I told her that when we get to heaven we will get to fly and we will get to ride a flying horse. And, if you need it really badly, I think Jesus might be willing to put a horn on your horse. Seriously, there is no way for me to promise this young woman a unicorn, but I can promise her a flying horse and a part in the greatest battle the earth has ever seen. I can also promise her that she will survive the battle and will be on the winning side as a faithful follower of Jesus. To study our part in the second coming of Jesus, let us look more closely at the passage in Revelation 19.

An Army That Overcomes Opposition

In Revelation 2:25-26, Jesus encourages Christians, *"Only hold on to what you have until I come. To him who overcomes and does my will to the end, I will give authority over the nations…"* The promise of Jesus is to believers. If we will hold on to our faith in him, we will be given authority to rule with Jesus. That same passage continues in verse 27 and 28 saying,

> "'He will rule them with an iron scepter;
> he will dash them to pieces like pottery'— just as I [Jesus] have received authority from my Father. ²⁸I will also give him [the over comer] the morning star.

If we overcome the difficulties of this life, we will be given the opportunity to rule with Jesus in the future.

There are many rewards in heaven. However, possibly the greatest rewards are the opportunities that believers are given to work for the Lord in the future. In Matthew 25:21 and 23 Jesus offers the same words of recognition and promise to the two servants who invested their talents and made them fruitful. He says twice, *'Well done, good and faithful servant! You have been faithful with a few things; <u>I will put you in charge of many things.</u> Come and share your master's happiness!'* What was the reward for the servants? For the one who invested five talents to produce five more there was the gift of one talent[1], and for both of these servants there was the promise of greater trust, authority and opportunity for service in the future. In the King James Version, the words of promise in verses 21 and 23 are, *"I will make you ruler over many things."*

Luke 16:10-12 seems to restate the same principle in Jesus' teachings on the way we handle money, position, and power in this life.

> "Whoever can be trusted with very little can also be trusted with much, and whoever is dishonest with very little will also be dishonest with much. ¹¹So if you have not been trustworthy in handling worldly wealth, who will trust you with true riches? ¹²And if you have not been trustworthy with someone else's property, who will give you property of your own?

If we want to be rewarded in the future with opportunities to serve the Lord, to rule and reign with him, then we must be faithful in the little things we are given now. If I am unfaithful in serving as a volunteer in my church, following God's financial plans and witnessing to the lost now, what will I be trusted with in the future? I am not serving Jesus because I am afraid of him. I am serving him because I am motivated to prepare my heart, mind, sprit and attitude to rule and reign with him in the future. Today is the training camp for ruling and reigning with him. My performance, which is only accomplished by his grace and power mixed with my willingness, will determine my reward in the future. The reward will, in many ways, be further opportunities to serve!

So, if this is the reward that is promised to overcomers, I want to be an overcomer. I will not give the devil a foothold.[2] I will serve Christ in the face of opposition and resistance. I will overcome, depending completely upon God's strength. When I am willing to follow, God's strength will help me overcome every difficulty that the devil, the world, and those who hate God can throw at me! I will be in the army of overcomers!

One question that you may be asking at this point is, how do I know that this army is made of believers and not angels? How do I know that I will be in that army of overcomers? As we look at Revelation 19, we are given a description of the members of the army that follows Jesus at his return. Revelation 19:14 says, *"The armies of heaven were following him, riding on white horses and dressed in fine linen, white and clean."* So who are these who are riding on white horses and dressed in fine linen that is white and clean? We find the answer in two other passages of Revelation. Revelation 7:9 says,

> *"After this I looked and there before me was a great multitude that no one could count, from every nation, tribe, people and language, standing before the throne and in front of the Lamb. They were wearing white robes and were holding palm branches in their hands."*

Then also in Revelation 7:15, we get another hint,

> *"And he said, "These are they who have come out of the great tribulation; they have washed their robes and made them white in the blood of the Lamb. Therefore, "they are before the throne of God and serve him day and night in his temple; and he who sits on the throne will spread his tent over them."*

In other parts of Revelation, the individuals who are given robes that are white are believers. In Revelation 3:4, Jesus describes those who walk with him as dressed in white. In Revelation 3:18, the encouragement of Jesus to the church at Laodicea is to buy, *"white clothes to wear."* The picture all through the New Testament concerning clothing is that believers are clothed in the righteousness of Christ.[3] In 2 Corinthians 5, Paul discusses the believers' future glorification in body and uses the picture of putting off the current tent we live in to be clothed in a new body.[4] There are instances where angels are described as dressed in white, but the bulk of Revelation indicates that those dressed in white are believers who overcame by the power of God in this life and are receiving their reward.

The encouragement is simply this, be an overcomer. Overcome in the battles with temptation that you face. Overcome in the battles you face in ministry in this life. First, overcome by holding on to what you have. Do not lose spiritual ground to Satan. Second, overcome by investing your talents and resources in the kingdom of God so that you will present him with your profitable increase when he returns for you. There is an amazing reward and opportunity given to those who overcome.

An Army That Overpowers Oppressors

Revelation 19:19, we see the enemies of this great army of Christ's followers. *"Then I saw the beast and the kings of the earth and their armies gathered together to make war against the rider on the horse and his army."* The enemies of the army of heaven are the antichrist, the beast, and the nations and armies that are allied with him. In chapter three, we looked briefly at the person known as the antichrist and the spirit of antichrist that is in the world right now. It is described in 1 Thessalonians 2:6-7. With the church raptured, that is, caught away to heaven by Jesus, the spirit of antichrist is given nearly complete freedom to rule the world and he does. The antichrist has all political power on the earth after the rapture of the church during the seven year tribulation. His side kick, so to speak, is the beast. The beast is a religious leader who persuades the world to follow and even worship the antichrist through many means, one of which is counterfeit miracles.

The beast's ability to perform miracles should not make you think that all miracles are counterfeit and empowered by some cultic or satanic power. There are miracles today that are empowered by Satan. Consider the stories of demonic possession, oppression and sickness in the gospels. The man who was mute[5], the woman who was bent over[6], the boy that threw himself in the fire[7], the pigs that committed suicide[8], are all miracles of Satan. But Jesus also indicated that we can expect good, divine miracles from God! If we have faith, we can tell a mountain to move[9] or an olive tree to be uprooted and replanted[10]. If we lay hands on the sick they will recover[11]. As New Testament believers we are commanded to pray for miracles and trust God for results in Jesus' name. In time of spiritual warfare, we can trust God to overcome the powers of the devil and his counterfeit miracles.

What are some of the marks of the spirit of antichrist? One, there is a desire to eradicate Israel and the Jewish people. We see this spirit in several places in history, in the reign of King Xerxes in the Persian Empire[12], in the wars of Antiochus Epiphanes against Judea, and even more recently in the Nazi attempt to eradicate Jews. In Revelation 12, we see the final attempt of the antichrist to eradicate the Jewish people. If God cannot keep his promise to the Jewish people and to Abraham, then he is not all powerful, nor is he a holy being able to keep his own word and promises. Two, the spirit of antichrist is just what the name implies; it is a spirit fighting against the work and person of Jesus Christ. This would mean that the spirit of antichrist is working against the redemption plan of God through Jesus, the individual redemption of people through Jesus, the truth of Jesus' sinless life, divinity, virgin birth and physical resurrection from the dead. Sadly, the spirit of antichrist is actually working in some so-called Christian denominations of churches.

In the history of the world, we have seen dictatorial rulers many times. However, this ruler will be the most dictatorial of all that have come before.

First, this will be a ruler who rules the entire world. There will be no other option or choice to follow. If all nations are united in following him, what country would be available for his detractors to flee to? Second, he will have complete control over the economic system. If you do not take his mark of allegiance, you will not be able to buy or sell anything. Third, he will hold complete religious power and ultimately require the world to worship him. His rule is oppressive to say the least. It may seem far-fetched to many, but for those who are serving Jesus, the writing on the wall can already be seen. The culture of religious and moral tolerance in America is already coming to a point that restricts religious freedoms. The move toward unification of the world economy is in motion. The uniting of nations into a global organization under global law also shows us that globalization, though helpful in many respects, can also prepare the way for this oppressive world ruler.

So who does this army of believers led by Jesus overcome in this giant battle? The army overcomes the greatest oppressor of humanity in all of history. The antichrist is defeated by this army of overcomers. If you have a passion for social justice, become a Christian. God wants to use you now to promote truthful, scientifically and psychologically sound morals in this world. Then, in the future, you will be a part of the greatest overthrow of the greatest human oppression ever seen on the planet!

An Army That Abducts the Antichrist

Revelation 19:20 tells us about the end of the battle, the winning side, and the prisoners of war.

> *"But the beast was captured, and with him the false prophet who had performed the miraculous signs on his behalf. With these signs he had deluded those who had received the mark of the beast and worshiped his image. The two of them were thrown alive into the fiery lake of burning sulfur."*

At the end of the battle, the beast and the false prophet that performs miracles for the beast are captured and thrown into the lake of fire. Interestingly, the place where Satan and the wicked dead are judged for eternity, which is the lake of fire, will be inhabited first by the antichrist and his religious sidekick, the false prophet. We often hear prophecy teachers speak about the horrible power and authority of the antichrist in terrifying terms. For those who remain on the earth for the tribulation, his power is horrible. But, for believers who were a part of the resurrection of the church or the rapture of the church, the antichrist is a defeated enemy. We are in the army that takes the antichrist as a P.O.W!

An Army That Wields the Word

In the depiction of the army that follows Jesus, there is only one weapon mentioned. Revelation 19:21 says, *"The rest of them were killed with the sword that came out of the mouth of the rider on the horse, and all the birds gorged themselves on their flesh."* The only weapon mentioned is the sword that comes out of the mouth of the rider on the white horse. The rider on the white horse is Jesus Christ the Lord, whose word created the world.[13] Jesus is the only one mentioned as striking the nations and creating destruction. Jesus is the violent one in the picture John gives in Revelation 19. Notice that Jesus' robe is dipped in blood (Revelation 19:13). In Isaiah 63:1-6, Isaiah prophesies about two future events.

> *1 Who is this coming from Edom,*
> *from Bozrah, with his garments stained crimson?*
> *Who is this, robed in splendor,*
> *striding forward in the greatness of his strength?*
> *"It is I, speaking in righteousness,*
> *mighty to save."*
> *2 Why are your garments red,*
> *like those of one treading the winepress?*
> *3 "I have trodden the winepress alone;*
> *from the nations no one was with me.*
> *I trampled them in my anger*
> *and trod them down in my wrath;*
> *their blood spattered my garments,*
> *and I stained all my clothing.*
> *4 For the day of vengeance was in my heart,*
> *and the year of my redemption has come.*
> *5 I looked, but there was no one to help,*
> *I was appalled that no one gave support;*
> *so my own arm worked salvation for me,*
> *and my own wrath sustained me.*
> *6 I trampled the nations in my anger;*
> *in my wrath I made them drunk*
> *and poured their blood on the ground."*

Look at these features. First, Isaiah asks, "Who is coming from Edom…?" Jesus and his army will approach Jerusalem and the Battle of Armageddon from the east. Second, Isaiah says, "I have trodden the winepress alone…" Jesus was alone at Calvary. Third, "For the day of vengeance was in my heart…" Jesus, alone on the cross looked forward to the day of vengeance to come when his clothing would be stained with the blood of his destroyed enemies.

The sword that comes out of Jesus' mouth is the Word of God. Hebrews tells us that the Word of God is a sword. And, Galatians tells us that the sword of the spirit is the word of God when describing the armor of God. Also, Revelation 4 pictures Jesus with a sword in his mouth. Finally, the Word is pictured here again as a sword. He will destroy the nations that follow the beast with the word of his mouth, the Word of God. We need to realize more fully the power of the Word of God. We need to pray it, memorize it, and read it. Hide it in our hearts.

An Army That is Enlisting Immediately!

If you want to be in the army that is riding on white horses, you should enlist now. Accept Jesus as your Savior and Lord. If you want to be on the side that is fighting and losing on the ground, there is nothing you need to do. If you have not chosen Jesus Christ, you are already on their side. The good news is you can change sides right now! You are not doomed to lose, and God is calling you to be on his side, the side of his Son, Jesus Christ.

In Psalm 2:9, David writes about Jesus destroying his enemies in preparation for his rule of the earth. *"You will rule them with an iron scepter; you will dash them to pieces like pottery."* We see from verse two, that David is speaking of Jesus Christ (Christ translated is "Anointed one") destroying his enemies. Consider the context of this promise from the Psalms (underlined emphasis mine).

> *¹ Why do <u>the nations conspire</u>*
>   *and <u>the peoples plot in vain</u>?*
> *² <u>The kings of the earth take their stand</u>*
>   *<u>and the rulers gather together</u>*
>   *<u>against the LORD</u>*
>   *<u>and against his Anointed One</u>.*

> ³ *"Let us break their chains,"* they say,
>   *"and throw off their fetters."*
> ⁴ *The One enthroned in heaven laughs;*
>   *the Lord scoffs at them.*
> ⁵ *Then he rebukes them in his anger*
>   *and terrifies them in his wrath, saying,*
> ⁶ *"I have installed my King*
>   *on Zion, my holy hill."*
> ⁷ *I will proclaim the decree of the LORD :*
>   *He said to me, "You are my Son ;*
>   *today I have become your Father.*
> ⁸ *Ask of me,*
>   *<u>and I will make the nations your inheritance,</u>*
>   *<u>the ends of the earth your possession.</u>*
> ⁹ *<u>You will rule them with an iron scepter ;</u>*
>   *<u>you will dash them to pieces like pottery</u>."*
> ¹⁰ *Therefore, you kings, be wise;*
>   *be warned, you rulers of the earth.*
> ¹¹ *Serve the LORD with fear*
>   *and rejoice with trembling.*
> ¹² *Kiss the Son, lest he be angry*
>   *and you be destroyed in your way,*
>   *for his wrath can flare up in a moment.*
>   *Blessed are all who take refuge in him.*

Today is the day to kiss the Son. Today is the day for you to join Jesus' side. Today is the day to enlist in Jesus' service and choose to be on the winning side when this world system is brought to an end. Think about God's unbelievable grace! Think about his power to change our hearts! He can transform his enemies into friends. He wants to make you a winner, not a loser. As he promised in Deuteronomy 28, you will be at the top and not the bottom, the head and not the tail. God loves you so much he is asking you to enlist with him today.

---

[1] Matthew 25:28
[2] Ephesians 4:27

[3] Galatians 3:27 *"...all of you who were baptized into Christ have clothed yourselves with Christ."*
[4] 2 Corinthians 5:2-4
[5] Mark 9:25
[6] Luke 13:11
[7] Matthew 7:14-16
[8] Matthew 8:32
[9] Mark 11:23
[10] Luke 17:6
[11] Mark 16:18
[12] The book of Esther is about the aversion of this attempted Jewish holocaust.
[13] John 1:3

Chapter 6
"The Meek Shall Inherit the Earth."
The believer's part in the millennium

One of the most confusing scripture passages for me as a young believer was in Matthew 5 in the Sermon on the Mount. Jesus said, "Blessed are the meek, for they will inherit the earth." As a new believer in high school, I wondered, how could the meek gain all the property? Property is usually gained by economic power or by military force. A long time ago I listened to a cassette tape of a sermon by an old time preacher from Texas in which he mentioned this passage. He said that the Greek word for meek here is the word Romans used for a well tempered, well broken horse of war. The Greek word is *praÿs*, (pronounced *prä-ü's*) which can mean meek, mild or gentle. Jesus described himself this way in Matthew 21:5 when he rode into Jerusalem on a donkey. The meek are people with a certain disposition toward God; those who are easily directed by him, as if broken like a well trained horse. So, who inherits the earth? Those who have a meek disposition toward God. Those who are willing and practiced at following his commands and directions.

Once the battle of Armageddon is over, Christ and his army that follows him set up the kingdom of Christ on earth. Sound crazy? If you have ever sung the Hallelujah Chorus you have sung about it. *"The kingdoms of this world is become the kingdoms of our Lord, and of his Christ; and he shall reign for ever and ever."* It is a quotation from Revelation 11:15. Just read what happens after the battle in Revelation chapter 20.

> *[1]And I saw an angel coming down out of heaven, having the key to the Abyss and holding in his hand a great chain. [2]He seized the dragon, that ancient serpent, who is the devil, or Satan, and bound him for a thousand years. [3]He threw him into the Abyss, and locked and sealed it over him, to keep him from deceiving the nations anymore until the thousand years were ended. After that, he must be set free for a short time.*
> *[4]I saw thrones on which were seated those who had been given authority to judge. And I saw the souls of those who had been beheaded because of their testimony for Jesus and because of the word of God. They had not worshiped the beast or his image and had not received his mark on their foreheads or their hands. They came to life and reigned with Christ a thousand years. [5](The rest of the dead did not come to life until the thousand years were ended.) This is the first resurrection. [6]Blessed and holy are those who have part in the first resurrection. The second death has no power over them, but they will be priests of God and of Christ and will reign with him for a thousand years.*
> *[7]When the thousand years are over, Satan will be released from his prison [8]and will go out to deceive the nations in the four corners of the earth—Gog and Magog—to gather them for battle. In number they are like the sand on the seashore. [9]They marched across the breadth of the earth and surrounded the camp of God's people, the city he loves. But fire came down from heaven and devoured them. [10]And the devil, who deceived them, was thrown into the lake of burning sulfur, where the beast and the false prophet had been thrown. They will be tormented day and night for ever and ever.*

Satan Seized and Restricted Rev. 20:1-3

The first event in Jesus' reign on the earth is the capture and arrest of Satan. What a massive change this will be for reality as we know it! Just imagine if Satan were unable to do his work in the realm of the earth. One of the main changes that we will experience during this time is the opportunity to watch natural humanity function on earth in the presence of Christ and the absence of

Satan. I say that we will have the opportunity to watch because we will already be glorified and changed, we will no longer be natural humanity. The real relief will be for those who had been living in the tribulation under the restrictions and reign of the antichrist. Now they are not only free from his tyranny, but they are also free from the bothers of Satan. The antichrist has been thrown in the lake of fire and Satan is bound.

The Power of God's Angels.

Notice that an angel has a chain to capture Satan. It is some kind of unusual chain if it can bind an angel and so we are not given the complete description of how Satan is bound. Satan is a fallen angel. He is not equal in power to God. God is eternal and creator. Satan is not eternal. He is created and also fallen. In some religions, good and evil are considered as equal forces in the universe working against each other to hold things together. In some cults, Satan is described as Jesus' brother or some type of equal. Nothing could be further from the truth. God is all powerful and Satan, though powerful, is limited in power.

Remember that through God and the work of his son Jesus, we have authority over the devil. Just as this angel will be given ultimate authority to capture Satan and bind him, we have been given authority to overcome all the influence of the devil through the word of God and the authority of Christ. A good reason to have a consistent prayer and Bible study habit is to handle the word of God accurately through study, and know Jesus through prayer. Not that we rejoice in having power over the devil, our greatest joy knowing that we are saved and now on God's side!

The Place of Satan's Arrest.

John tells us that Satan is thrown into the abyss. This is not his final place of eternal punishment. It seems to be the space between heaven and hell. Some vast no-mans land if you will. It is called the abyss apparently because it is some type of chasm in between. Wherever and whatever it is, it is sufficient to hold Satan for a long time. Remember, the antichrist and the beast have already been cast into the lake of fire. Satan is not placed there since he will be released for a season. It is important to note that once a person or angel is cast into the lake of fire, there is absolutely no leaving that place. People will not be saved out of the lake of fire. Choose Christ today, there is no turning back later. In the next chapter we will explore the New Heavens and the New Earth. However, there is no new lake of fire. It is what it is.

The Peace in Satan's Absence.

During the 1,000 year reign, Satan will not be free to deceive. Deception is the primary tool of the devil. Other than lies, he has no real power. Through his lies he causes us to doubt God's existence, God's Word, God's power, God's intentions, and his promises to us. In Genesis 3, Satan tempted Adam and Eve. His tool was not the tree or the fruit. The tool was deception. Read this chapter carefully for yourself and you will see that he caused the couple to doubt God's word, his promises, his intentions, and his love for people. In the absence of these lies, there will be great peace and prosperity on the earth, even though it is the same earth that we live in now with all its faults and curses. Mankind will still wrestle with the sinful nature and the flesh, but it will be greatly alleviated with the binding of Satan and his inability to deceive.

Saints Seated and Ruling Rev. 20:4-6

The Participants in the First Resurrection

Revelation 20:4-6 says, *"They came to life and reigned with Christ a thousand years… This is the first resurrection."* Those who are ruling are the ones who were in the first resurrection. Jesus explained the two resurrections in John 5:28-29, *"Do not be amazed at this, for a time is coming when all who are in their graves will hear his voice and come out—those who have done good will rise to live, and those who have done evil will rise to be condemned."* Jesus indicates that all humans will rise from the grave at one time or another according to God's plan.

In 1 Thessalonians 4, we find a resurrection of believers, the blessed hope. In Revelation 20:4-6, we see that believers who were killed for their faith during the tribulation are graciously raised to rule with the saints who were raised at the time of the blessed hope. Remember, the blessed hope is the believers' resurrection and the rapture of the Church. So, all who placed their faith in Jesus in history will be raised to reign with him. All these raised believers constitute the first resurrection. In Revelation 20:11-15, we see the general resurrection of all the dead. Even the wicked dead will rise, but only to be judged and sent with Satan into the lake of fire. What a despicable situation! To experience life in the body again for a moment only to be cast body and soul into the lake of fire where the punishment will be spiritual but also physical for all eternity. Hell is the absence of God's presence, but it is also literal physical punishment forever. There are two resurrections; you want to be in the first!

Those who are ruling in the thousand year reign are all those who make up the redeemed people of God, from Adam and Eve to the battle of Armageddon. Old Testament saints, New Testament saints and tribulation saints. What an amazing thought to have the opportunity to work along side the great individuals of the faith through the ages.

The Prerogatives of the Faithful to Reign

The main question of this book is how will we live then, meaning how shall we live in eternity? What will we be doing and what will we be like? At this point in prophetic history, during the 1,000 year reign of Christ, the picture is drastically different and equally exciting. The Bible actually gives us a number of hints about this future time that answers our main question.

One hint is that the capital city of the world will be Jerusalem. And nations will travel in and out of it and the laws of the kingdom will come from that location. Isaiah 2:2-4 tells us about this time.

> *² In the last days*
> *the mountain of the LORD's temple will be established*
> *as chief among the mountains;*
> *it will be raised above the hills,*
> *and all nations will stream to it.*
> *³ Many peoples will come and say,*
> *"Come, let us go up to the mountain of the LORD,*
> *to the house of the God of Jacob.*
> *He will teach us his ways,*

> *so that we may walk in his paths."*
> *The law will go out from Zion,*
> *the word of the LORD from Jerusalem.*
> *⁴ He will judge between the nations*
> *and will settle disputes for many peoples.*
> *They will beat their swords into plowshares*
> *and their spears into pruning hooks.*
> *Nation will not take up sword against nation,*
> *nor will they train for war anymore.*

The reason that Jesus will rule in Jerusalem is because it is the city that God chose for David and his descendants to rule,[1] and because that is the place where God placed his temple, his house that bore his name[2]. Today, the world is filled with disputes that often are centuries old. Many of those disputes and others that may still arise will be settled by Jesus. Micah 4:3-5 foretells this ministry of making peace that Jesus will have on the earth.

> *"³ He will judge between many peoples*
> *and will settle disputes for strong nations far and wide.*
> *They will beat their swords into plowshares*
> *and their spears into pruning hooks.*
> *Nation will not take up sword against nation,*
> *nor will they train for war anymore.*
> *⁴ Every man will sit under his own vine*
> *and under his own fig tree,*
> *and no one will make them afraid,*
> *for the LORD Almighty has spoken."*

It is no wonder that Jesus is called *"The Prince of Peace"* in Isaiah chapter nine. Jesus will be the ruler who brings world peace. We as resurrected believers will reign with him in his administration. There is no way to know exactly what that work will entail. Remember that at this time we will be glorified and will have spent seven years in heaven before returning to earth. We should not think that is completely unusual. Jesus himself will be returning in body having been glorified in heaven. We are simply being like him. We were buried with him through baptism. We live with him through the resurrection. We will reign with him. Living on earth in our glorified bodies will be another way in which we will identify with Christ as our Lord and leader.

The Promises of the Father Realized

There are several promises of God that will be completely realized in this time when Jesus reigns on the earth. Many promises in the Scriptures that we think of as figurative may be met literally in the millennial reign.

First, Israel will rule Palestine. In Genesis 15:18, God promised Abraham and his descendants the land of Palestine. *"On that day the LORD made a covenant with Abram and said, "To your descendants I give this land, from the river of Egypt to the great river, the Euphrates."* In the millennium, Jesus will completely fulfill that promise to Abraham's descendants.

Second, David will be Jesus' second in command. Ezekiel 35:22-24 says, *"I will save my flock, and they will no longer be plundered. I will judge between one sheep and another. ^{23}I will place over them one shepherd, my servant David, and he will tend them; he will tend them and be their shepherd. ^{24}I the LORD will be their God, and my servant David will be prince among them. I the LORD have spoken."* We don't know all the details about Jesus' administration, but we do know that David will be second in command.

Third, the Apostles will judge or rule Israel. Jesus promised this in Luke 22:28-30. *"You are those who have stood by me in my trials. ^{29}And I confer on you a kingdom, just as my Father conferred one on me, ^{30}so that you may eat and drink at my table* *in my kingdom and sit on thrones, judging the twelve tribes of Israel."* Have you ever wondered why the twelve apostles were all Jews? First because God said that through Abraham all nations on earth would be blessed. Through Jesus, a Jew, and his Apostles, also all Jews, the gospel went to the Jew first, and then it went to the whole world, the Gentiles. Also because they will judge the twelve tribes of which they are a part.

Fourth, the saints will have authority to rule. Revelation 3:21 says, *"To him who overcomes, I will give the right to sit with me on my throne, just as I overcame and sat down with my Father on his throne."* We do not have the exact details of what ruling entails. It will mean that the saints will be working for Jesus as he leads the world. Jesus quotes the master in the parable of the talents. In Matthew 25:21, the master only says, *"Well done, good and faithful servant! You have been faithful with a few things; I will put you in charge of many things."* It is interesting how Luke 19:17 records Jesus as saying, *"'Well done, my good servant!' his master replied. 'Because you have been trustworthy in a very small matter, take charge of ten cities."* It may be that those who are faithful will literally rule geographic regions such as cities. I had some Bible college professors who had joked about which cites would be placed in their charge.

Fifth, the creation will be at peace. This is not the complete peace that will be realized in the New Heavens and the New Earth. We will look at this in the next chapter. But, with Jesus, the Prince of Peace and creator of the world at the wheel, the world will have an opportunity for ecological health like we have never seen in our time.

Look at Isaiah 35 with me.

> *¹The desert and the parched land will be glad;*
> *the wilderness will rejoice and blossom.*
> *Like the crocus, ² it will burst into bloom;*
> *it will rejoice greatly and shout for joy.*
> *The glory of Lebanon will be given to it,*
> *the splendor of Carmel and Sharon;*
> *they will see the glory of the LORD,*
> *the splendor of our God.*

Middle Eastern deserts will be restored to the foliage that previously was there. Much of the over-use of the Fertile Crescent and Palestine will be healed when Jesus directs healing ecological policy. Is there a place for the Christian ecologist? Yes! It is the plan of Jesus for this earth to be healthy even though it is under the curse of sin caused by humanity who has dominion over it. Let's continue in Isaiah 35.

> *³ Strengthen the feeble hands,*
> *steady the knees that give way;*
> *⁴ say to those with fearful hearts,*
> *"Be strong, do not fear;*
> *your God will come,*
> *he will come with vengeance;*
> *with divine retribution*
> *he will come to save you."*
> *⁵ Then will the eyes of the blind be opened*
> *and the ears of the deaf unstopped.*

There will be healing for the sick and those whose bodies are still frustrated by the cursed earth. If Jesus is the same yesterday, today and forever, then he is still a healing Lord and will be when he reigns on the earth. We will be a part of a standard of health in the millennium that will be unequaled in earth's history. Later, in the New Heavens and the New Earth, all things will be made new and healing will not even be needed.

> *⁶ Then will the lame leap like a deer,*
>   *and the mute tongue shout for joy.*
>   *Water will gush forth in the wilderness*
>   *and streams in the desert.*
> *⁷ The burning sand will become a pool,*
>   *the thirsty ground bubbling springs.*
>   *In the haunts where jackals once lay,*
>   *grass and reeds and papyrus will grow.*
> *⁸ And a highway will be there;*
>   *it will be called the Way of Holiness.*
>   *The unclean will not journey on it;*
>   *it will be for those who walk in that Way;*
>   *wicked fools will not go about on it.*
> *⁹ No lion will be there,*
>   *nor will any ferocious beast get up on it;*
>   *they will not be found there.*
>   *But only the redeemed will walk there,*
> *¹⁰ and the ransomed of the LORD will return.*
>   *They will enter Zion with singing;*
>   *everlasting joy will crown their heads.*
>   *Gladness and joy will overtake them,*
>   *and sorrow and sighing will flee away.*

Sixth, the wisdom of Christ will be revealed. Isaiah 11:9 looks forward to this day when the knowledge of the Lord will fill the earth.

> *⁹ They will neither harm nor destroy*
>   *on all my holy mountain,*
>   *for the earth will be full of the knowledge of the LORD*
>   *as the waters cover the sea.*

St. Augustine said, "All truth is God's truth." When Jesus stood before Pilate he described his reason for entering the world, to *"testify to the truth."* Jesus embodies truth. Not just religious truth and philosophical truth, but the truth in every area of life.

Satan Seduces and Rebels Rev. 20:7-10

You think that after all that God has done at this point in time that Satan would give up. If he did not give up after God fulfilled Old Testament promises about Jesus work on the cross, he will not give up even after God fulfills New Testament promises about Jesus coming again.

Satan's Persistence and Determination

A pastor was amazed at a woman in his church that always had positive things to say about everyone. He was pleased, but began to wonder if she was simply dishonest at some point by never having any critique of anyone or anything. One Sunday the pastor needed to teach the Sunday school class she attended because her regular teacher was out of town. The subject was Satan. One of the discussion questions was, "What do you think of the devil?" He thought she would have something negative to say. The pastor was surprised to hear her say of Satan, "Well, at least he is persistent."

Amazingly, at the end of the 1,000 year reign of Christ, Satan is released from his bondage in the abyss and he immediately begins his work of deception and temptation. His goal is to drive people as far from God as possible. Revelation 12 tells us that he is filled with rage because he knows his time is short. Fueled by rage, Satan is determined to take as much from God as possible. You might think 999 years wrapped in a chain living in an abyss might cool Satan off, but it will not. He will still be filled with rage.

Satan's Power to Deceive (Rev. 20:8)

In Revelation 20:8 we see that Satan is released to do the work of deceiving the nations. Why would Satan be released? Here is a great description from

George Eldon Ladd. At his release, *"Satan will find the heart of men still responsive to his enticements even though they have lived in a period of peace and righteousness. This will serve to commend the justice of God in the final judgment. Sin -rebellion against God- is not due to an evil society or a bad environment."*[3] When we stand before God, we will not be able to blame anyone else or anything in our life. We are responsible for every act or lack of action. In the tribulation, the worst times of human history, people will be saved, place their faith in Jesus and live in obedience though it costs them their lives. Also, in the most perfect of times in the history of the earth since the fall of man, humanity will still be captivated by the deceit of Satan.

You might think that after 1,000 years of peace, health, and ecological prosperity under Jesus' rule that only a few would defect to Satan's side. But Revelation 20 says, *"In number the deceived are like the sand on the seashore."* Consider the potential of Satan to deceive! He deceives thousands upon thousands who have lived in the millennial reign!

Satan's Plan to Destroy (Rev. 20:9)

There seems to be a plan of attack by Satan and the nations of the world that he deceives into following him in this season at the end of the 1,000 years. First, they plan to move on the capital of Jesus' millennial kingdom, Jerusalem. It is hard to understand what they think they will accomplish. Jesus and the saints have all been raised from the dead and according to 1 Corinthians 15, are immortal. Apparently, there is some goal to kill key players that would fulfill the promises of God. It has been Satan's plan for centuries to keep God from fulfilling his promise by killing key players. If Satan can kill the key players, essential characters, who are the recipients of the promises then the promise can not be kept. In Esther, Satan tried to wipe out the Jews a group God chose to make essential. In the gospels, Satan tried to kill Jesus first as a baby in Bethlehem, then on a temple pinnacle during his temptation, both would have been premature causing some or all of God's promises to be missed. Assuming the typical mode of operation of Satan, this will again be the plan. His plan will again include wrecking God's purposes in the lives of individuals he deceives. He is doing that work today and will continue his work fueled by rage upon his release.

At this time, we will not be able to be deceived. Since we have been glorified at the resurrection/rapture, we will not be the ones who fall for Satan's lies. The nations of the earth at the end of the 1,000 years are the descendants of people who survived the seven year tribulation and the Battle of Armageddon. It seems strange to us now to think of Jesus literally ruling the world. But, we must remember that God's revelation to man since the fall in Genesis 3 has been an increasing revelation. God spoke to Abraham, one man, then to Israel, one nation, then to a region of nations at the dispersion of the Jews. Next, God spoke to the whole world through the revelation of his Son into the world. God literally injected his divine Son into the world for a brief time already. Jesus returning to earth at his second coming is another step in God revealing himself more fully to the world. Each time we have a fuller description of who God is and what his plan is all about.

Satanic Provokers Devoured (Rev. 20:9)

The end of Satan's revolt is described by John. The armies of Satan are destroyed by fire and Satan is thrown into the lake of fire. We get to witness this great event. There is no description of our part in this struggle. Assuming that the saints are distributed throughout the earth ruling and reigning, we will have some part in opposing the deceptions of Satan, but the destruction of his armies seems to be all God's work. Just as in the destruction of the nations in the battle of Armageddon, God alone holds the power to destroy natural unredeemed men. Jesus said, *"Do not judge, or you too will be judged...."*[4] When it comes to destroying people in these last battles, God seems to hold that authority to himself. This is not to say that God has not used people to exercise deadly judgment on other people. He used Assyria to execute judgment on Israel[5] and in Revelation he used people against people to execute judgment.[6]

---

[1] 2 Samuel 5:7
[2] 1 Kings 8:43
[3] Clouse, Robert G. Editor, *The Meaning of the Millennium: Four Views.* Quoted form the chapter written by George Eldon Ladd. (Doners Grove, IL: InterVarsity Press, 1977) p. 40.
[4] Matthew 7:1
[5] Isaiah 7:18; 20; 8:1
[6] Revelation 6:8

Chapter 7
Forever
Living in Eternity

As we have begun to see in this book, the simple answer to, "what happens to a believer when we die?" has traditionally been, believers go to Heaven. However true, it is a very simplified answer that does not tell the whole story. If I died today I would go to Heaven and be with the Lord, but there is still at least 1007 years of adventure serving Jesus before we reach the final state of Heaven. The final state of believers in eternity is what the Bible calls, *"The New Heavens and the New Earth."* It is at this point that we and the creation have reached the full redemption of God. Let's look at the Scripture's description that is given to us in Revelation 20:11-21:8.

> Then I saw a great white throne and him who was seated on it. Earth and sky fled from his presence, and there was no place for them. [12]And I saw the dead, great and small, standing before the throne, and books were opened. Another book was opened, which is the book of life. The dead were judged according to what they had done as recorded in the books. [13]The sea gave up the dead that were in it, and death and Hades gave up the dead that were in them, and each person was judged according to what he had done. [14]Then death and Hades were thrown into the lake of fire. The lake of fire is the second death. [15]If anyone's name was not found written in the book of life, he was thrown into the lake of fire.

¹Then I saw a new heaven and a new earth, for the first heaven and the first earth had passed away, and there was no longer any sea. ²I saw the Holy City, the new Jerusalem, coming down out of heaven from God, prepared as a bride beautifully dressed for her husband. ³And I heard a loud voice from the throne saying, "Now the dwelling of God is with men, and he will live with them. They will be his people, and God himself will be with them and be their God. ⁴He will wipe every tear from their eyes. There will be no more death or mourning or crying or pain, for the old order of things has passed away."

⁵He who was seated on the throne said, "I am making everything new!" Then he said, "Write this down, for these words are trustworthy and true."

⁶He said to me: "It is done. I am the Alpha and the Omega, the Beginning and the End. To him who is thirsty I will give to drink without cost from the spring of the water of life. ⁷He who overcomes will inherit all this, and I will be his God and he will be my son. ⁸But the cowardly, the unbelieving, the vile, the murderers, the sexually immoral, those who practice magic arts, the idolaters and all liars—their place will be in the fiery lake of burning sulfur. This is the second death."

If you read Genesis chapters one through three you will find many of the same themes and ideas that are found in Revelation twenty one and twenty two. Some of the similarities are the presence of divine light without the sun or moon, the tree of life that gives eternal life and the presence of God with mankind. In Genesis, God creates time, "there was evening and there was morning - the first day."[1] In Revelation, we find the beginning of eternity and time is no longer necessary, "There will be no more night."[2] Though there are several more similarities that we could examine, the main point is that Genesis chapters one through three and the last two chapters of Revelation are like bookends on a shelf. They bind the entire Bible story into one complete view of all of history. What God began in the Garden of Eden he will regain in the end. The work of God in saving mankind started in the Garden and will end when he restores all things, every believer is perfectly healed and the entire creation is healed as well. Redemption is not only for believers, it is for all creation. God made mankind to be perfect and live in a perfect world. That will be obtained in the New Heavens and the New Earth.

The Final Judgment Rev. 20:11-15

Before the New Heavens and the New Earth are introduced there is one final act of justice and judgment that must be accomplished. This is the final judgment, often called the Great White Throne judgment because of the throne that John describes at this time.[3] Hundreds of years before Christ, God also showed this end-time judgment to Daniel which is recorded in Daniel 12:2-4.

> *"Multitudes who sleep in the dust of the earth will awake: some to everlasting life, others to shame and everlasting contempt. ³Those who are wise will shine like the brightness of the heavens, and those who lead many to righteousness, like the stars for ever and ever. ⁴But you, Daniel, close up and seal the words of the scroll until the time of the end. Many will go here and there to increase knowledge."*

In Matthew 25:31-44 Jesus explains the event.

> *"³¹When the Son of Man comes in his glory, and all the angels with him, he will sit on his throne in heavenly glory. ³²All the nations will be gathered before him, and he will separate the people one from another as a shepherd separates the sheep from the goats. ³³He will put the sheep on his right and the goats on his left.*
> *³⁴"Then the King will say to those on his right, 'Come, you who are blessed by my Father; take your inheritance, the kingdom prepared for you since the creation of the world."*

It is Final Because there are Previous Judgments.

Not only is this called the Great White Throne judgment, it is also referred to as the final judgment. It is final, because there are other judgments before it. All through the Scriptures there have been smaller judgments. On an individual level God executes his judgment when he turns an individual over to do what they want and ceases to convict them of their sin.[4] If you are living in a situation where you feel no sorrow or guilt for things that the Bible calls sinful, you are already in a serious place of judgment. The worst judgment that you can experience right now is that God chooses to leave you alone. In this state, you will most certainly store up judgment for yourself by creating a long list of wrongs against God.[5]

God's judgment may also be displayed in small individual acts of wrath against those who are being disobedient to him. The Old Testament is filled with displays of God's judgment. The Old Testament covenant was one of law and punishment for breaking that law. The New Testament covenant is one of grace and mercy. The righteous requirements of God are no longer external rules but internal rules dealing with the attitude of the heart. Since, in the New Testament, God is working through grace, we see far fewer of these individual displays of wrath. However, with the inclusion of the story of Ananias and Sapphira in Acts 5, we must conclude that God can and may occasionally act in individual judgment in the New Testament.

Another judgment is made at the time of the rapture. God is the only divine being able to know who is to be taken and who is to be left. The judgment seat of Christ that is yet another time of judgment described in 2 Corinthians 5:10 where those raptured/resurrected, who are already accepted as redeemed, have their acts of service to the Lord judged for the receiving of rewards from God. Then there are the judgments of the seven year tribulation period. Though there are many judgments, some large and some small, the Great White Throne

Judgment will be the final judgment of God. After this, all that is not in the lake of fire will be eternally perfect.

All the Dead Will Rise

Here are the items that are clear to us. Everyone who has ever lived will rise from the dead to be judged. Will all people then rise from the dead at some point? Yes. But, we as believers will have already been raised in the first resurrection.[6] Imagine how despicable it will be to rise from the dead, living again briefly, only to be found guilty of an eternal crime, the rejection of God's one and only Son Jesus Christ. I did not make the rules, God made them. I trust in his unfailing love,[7] his mercy[8] and justice[9]. Based only on God's perfect qualities I can write with assurance that God will keep his promises in his word to condemn those who reject Jesus Christ to an eternity in the lake of fire. The encouragement of Scripture is to accept Jesus Christ as our Savior and Lord today. God sent his Son into the world, not to condemn the world, but to save it. Jesus was sent because God loved the world. As John 3:16 and 17 says,

> *[16]"For God so loved the world that he gave his one and only Son, that whoever believes in him shall not perish but have eternal life. [17]For God did not send his Son into the world to condemn the world, but to save the world through him."*

Because God is perfect in mercy and love, he sent his Son for all of us. Because of his perfect justice and judgment there must be a time when rejection of God's truth and eternal love will receive a response from God.

Are You Ready?

This may seem like a strange question at this point in the book. You have been reading about heaven and various promised acts of God's judgment for some time now. But maybe you have still been fighting the work that the Holy Spirit is doing in your heart as you read this book. Are you ready for the next step in your adventure with God? Are you ready to meet him when you die? Are you ready if Jesus were to return for the catching away of the church today? Now is the time to give everything to Jesus Christ. Now is the day to believe in Jesus' work on the cross and his resurrection from the grave. Today is the day to ask for forgiveness of sins and start living for him. Maybe you need to set this book down for a few minutes and talk to God right now. If you choose Christ right now, let me know! I want to celebrate with you!

The New Heavens and New Earth   Rev. 21:1-8

The Current Earth is Cursed and Waiting (Gen. 3:17; Romans 8:18-25).

Most of us think about nature in a pure way. We want to get away from all the noise of life and go to nature. Though we feel a sense of purity in nature, it is not the perfection that God created it to be in the beginning. Genesis 3:17 says,

> *"To Adam he said, "Because you listened to your wife and ate from the tree about which I commanded you, 'You must not eat of it,'*
> *"Cursed is the ground because of you;*
> *through painful toil you will eat of it*
> *all the days of your life.*

The purity of nature that we now see is actually tainted due to the sin of humanity being injected into the creation. If you read the creation story in Genesis, you will see that several things changed when the creation was cursed.

Work, which God made as a meaningful activity for man, became toil. The earth would not easily produce man's food. Also, thorns were introduced. The serpent or snake was given a new way of traveling. Often we think that creation is perfectly pristine and pure. However, it is not. It is longing for its redemption, the way God had originally designed it.

Paul tells us about the frustration and corruption of nature in Romans 8:18-25,

> [18]*I consider that our present sufferings are not worth comparing with the glory that will be revealed in us.* [19]*The creation waits in eager expectation for the sons of God to be revealed.* [20]*For the creation was subjected to frustration, not by its own choice, but by the will of the one who subjected it, in hope* [21]*that the creation itself will be liberated from its bondage to decay and brought into the glorious freedom of the children of God.*
> [22]*We know that the whole creation has been groaning as in the pains of childbirth right up to the present time.* [23]*Not only so, but we ourselves, who have the firstfruits of the Spirit, groan inwardly as we wait eagerly for our adoption as sons, the redemption of our bodies.* [24]*For in this hope we were saved. But hope that is seen is no hope at all. Who hopes for what he already has?* [25]*But if we hope for what we do not yet have, we wait for it patiently.*

The creation is waiting in eager expectation for our full salvation to be accomplished. When the creation is fully redeemed, we will also be fully redeemed. Think about the logic of it. After the rapture, we will have glorified bodies. But the creation will still be fallen. It will still not be a perfect situation for us. But when we live in the New Heaven and New Earth, even our setting will be perfect. We will examine this more in a few moments.

The Cursed Earth Will Be Dissolved

So, if God is making a New Heaven and New Earth, what will happen to the current cursed creation? The Bible actually speaks to this in several locations.

Check out these passages that describe some of the details about how the creation will be changed.

Isaiah 34:4
> ⁴ All the stars of the heavens will be dissolved
> and the sky rolled up like a scroll;
> all the starry host will fall
> like withered leaves from the vine,
> like shriveled figs from the fig tree.

Isaiah 66:22-24
> ²² "As the new heavens and the new earth that I make will endure before me," declares the LORD, "so will your name and descendants endure. ²³ From one New Moon to another and from one Sabbath to another, all mankind will come and bow down before me," says the LORD. ²⁴ "And they will go out and look upon the dead bodies of those who rebelled against me; their worm will not die, nor will their fire be quenched, and they will be loathsome to all mankind."

2 Peter 3:10-13
> ¹⁰But the day of the Lord will come like a thief. The heavens will disappear with a roar; the elements will be destroyed by fire, and the earth and everything in it will be laid bare. ¹¹Since everything will be destroyed in this way, what kind of people ought you to be? You ought to live holy and godly lives ¹²as you look forward to the day of God and speed its coming. That day will bring about the destruction of the heavens by fire, and the elements will melt in the heat. ¹³But in keeping with his promise we are looking forward to a new heaven and a new earth, the home of righteousness.

Revelation 20:11
> ¹¹Then I saw a great white throne and him who was seated on it. Earth and sky fled from his presence, and there was no place for them.

Psalm 102:25-27
> ²⁵ In the beginning you laid the foundations of the earth,
> and the heavens are the work of your hands.
> ²⁶ They will perish, but you remain;
> they will all wear out like a garment.
> Like clothing you will change them
> and they will be discarded.
> ²⁷ But you remain the same,
> and your years will never end.

Matthew 24:35
> ³⁵Heaven and earth will pass away, but my words will never pass away. (Also, Mark 13:31 and Luke 21:33)

One thing that the Bible is not clear about is where we will be during this change. Obviously, our physical bodies will have already changed. We will also be with God. We will be spectators of God's judgment at the end of the 1,000 year reign of Christ, but we will also observe God's creative work. We will be spectators at the recreation, or reforming of the creation! Have you ever thought how neat it would be to have seen the creation of the world? I can't wait to see it recreated!

The New Earth will Be Free From the Curse *(Revelation 21:4; 22:3; Isaiah 66:22-24; Isaiah 65:17-18).*

When the creation is remade it will be free from the curse of sin that is described in the early part of Genesis. Think about these two passages from Revelation. Revelation 21:4 says, *"He will wipe every tear from their eyes. There will be no more death or mourning or crying or pain, for the old order of things has passed away."* Also, Revelation 22:3 says, *"No longer will there be any curse. The throne of God and of the Lamb will be in the city, and his servants will serve him."*

Life will be completely different for us living in eternity in a natural world that is free from the curse of sin. The most obvious part of the curse is death. Revelation 21:4 says there will be no more death. We are not told all the scientific details of how this will be worked out. But neither were we told how creation worked in the garden prior to death. If we can believe that God created the world without death in the beginning, why is it so hard to think that he can't redeem the creation and restore it to its prior way of functioning?

Let your mind ponder this idea of no more death for a moment. What will we eat? The fruit from the tree of life will be replenished every month and Revelation tells us that its fruit is for the healing of the nations. Other than that, we don't know exactly what we will eat. If there is absolutely no more death, how will that affect cell multiplication in our bodies? Will things rot or ferment? Will we all be vegetarians in heaven? Isaiah 11:6 seems to indicate that some of the meat eating animals will become vegetarian in the New Earth.

> *6 The wolf will live with the lamb,*
> *the leopard will lie down with the goat,*
> *the calf and the lion and the yearling together;*
> *and a little child will lead them.*

There are untold changes when death is removed from all that is physical. Some of them are beyond our comprehension and ability to study because we have no way to experiment or observe outside of the current laws of the natural world. When the curse is removed, there are four things that will be eliminated: death, pain, toil and sin. Just thinking about the change in our existence with these four eliminated is mind boggling.

The Saints Rule With Christ Forever *(2 Timothy 2;12).*

2 Timothy 2:12 gives us a promise, *"...if we endure, we will also reign with him. If we disown him, he will also disown us..."* If we endure and keep our faith, we will be rewarded with the opportunity to reign with him. Because God gave Adam a task in the garden when everything was perfect, it will then follow that in the eternal state of the New Heavens and New Earth we will have a meaningful task from God. That task will not be toilsome. Imagine how true the words of

1 John 5:3 will be to us in eternity, *"And his commands are not burdensome..."* The current Earth will pass away, but as Jesus said, *"...my words will never pass away."* Even the Scriptures, which are true now, will be true then, and by the nature of our new eternal perspective take on a whole new depth of insight. We revel in the amazing fulfillment of Old Testament prophecies about Jesus coming to die for our sins. Imagine how much more amazing our view of Scripture will be when every promise has been fulfilled. When we reign with Christ in eternity, we will have as a reward for our faithfulness a meaningful task that will give us a sense of accomplishment, wonder, and adventure in heaven.

Jesus exemplifies the type of leadership that we will have when we reign with Christ. Reigning is not like what we think of now. As Jesus said, the kings of the earth *"lord it over them."*[10] The type of reign in heaven will be one of serving. Jesus said something strange to the disciples once (OK, maybe pretty often) when he said that when they reach heaven he would serve them.[11] We focus all our efforts on serving the Lord today, but when we get to heaven the Lord will reward us by serving us as we also serve him. If there is any administrative flow in the job duties of eternity, the one at the higher level will be serving more, not the other way around!

We Will Experience Eternal Increase *(Isaiah 9:7)*.

Most Christians are familiar with Isaiah chapter nine. It is also familiar to many as the source for the lyrics of Handle's *Hallelujah Chorus*. In Isaiah 9:7 there is an interesting insertion, *"Of the increase of his government and peace there will be no end."* In high school, a new believer was sitting with me at lunch and we were talking about our faith. She said, "I am afraid that heaven will be boring. If everything is perfect and everyone is saved, then there will be no change for eternity. If nothing changes forever I might get bored." My first thought was that for a new believer she sure is thinking a lot about her faith and future! But then, I began to wonder the same thing. How will we not get bored in heaven if the population is not growing and we are not growing and gaining something?

We do not know exactly what the increase may be in heaven, but there will be some increase. As we review all the things that God has done in time we will constantly be learning and praising God for his mighty acts and his minute acts of salvation. Today, there is no way to measure the number of things that God is doing for us right now. He is active everywhere, holding us together on the molecular level, moving the planets, and moving the direction of governments and nations to fulfill his salvation plan.

There will also be increase in our ability to admire the glory of God. There will no doubt be an increasing depth of worship as we interact with God, his angels and his saints who lived through the ages. Isaiah says that his peace will increase. What an amazing thought! What kind of peace will we have in heaven? Think of a baby as a "blank tablet"[12] (to coin a phrase from John Lock) with no cares, stress, or history of pain or suffering (or at least a lot less than an adult). We will have a peace better than a new born baby who is completely secure in his or her parents' embrace and care.

There are some who believe that the increase will be in population. I have heard some prophecy teachers teach this, but have never found it in writing. The idea is that the nations of the present earth, who serve the Lord through the millennium and repopulate the Earth following the tribulation (about ¾ of the earth is killed in that seven years), will continue as natural humans into eternity and will be able to increase in number. Some principals in Scripture seem to support this idea. God made man and told him to be fruitful and multiply and fill the earth. These would be people increasing in number as we do now, but never dying. We who have been saved by Christ would not be increasing in number, because Jesus said in Matthew 22 that we would neither marry or be given in marriage in heaven. Then Jesus says in verse 30, that we will be "like the angels." We will not be angels, remember from chapter one that God made us to be perfect humans. We will be like them, no longer involving ourselves in marriage or creating children.

On the other hand, this idea is not clearly identified in the Scriptures. Also, if the New Heavens and New Earth are remade and believers are glorified at the resurrection/rapture, then all humans would be transformed physically at the time of the New Heavens and New Earth. All created matter would be free from the curse, including any people.

Even if there is not a numerical increase in eternity there will be a growing increase in God's peace and majesty that will keep us in awe of him forever. We do not know all the ramifications of what the increase will be, but it seems to allow for some type of growth in our lives and relationship with God. Eternity will be static and unchanging since the setting will be perfection and perfect can not change or improve. However, we will forever be growing in our awe of God and in closeness to our infinite creator. What a great future!

---

[1] Genesis 1:5
[2] Revelation 22:5
[3] Revelation 20:11
[4] Romans 1:28
[5] Romans 2:5
[6] Revelation 20:5-6
[7] Exodus 15:13
[8] Nehemiah 9:31
[9] Psalm 9:8
[10] Matthew 20:25, Mark 10:42 and Luke 22:25
[11] Luke 12:35-38
[12] Sproul, R.C., *The Consequences of Ideas: Understanding the Concepts that Shaped Our World*, (Wheaton, IL: Crossway Books, 2000), 95.

Conclusions

What happens to believers when they die? We obviously don't know all the details. God has kept many of the particulars of our transition into eternity a secret. As I write, I am praying for a friend who has served the Lord for a lifetime, and now is in her late eighties. She is not only ready to go to heaven; she longs to go to heaven! In the last few weeks while she has been in the hospital she has been having dreams of going to heaven. Do we fail to dream about heaven because its reality is not rooted in our minds when we are awake? Though we don't know all the details, we do know that we serve a loving Heavenly Father who will care for us at all times. He promised to be with us, *"And surely I am with you always, to the very end of the age."*[1] Amazingly, the promise is to the end of the age, not to the end of our lives! God will be with you through the transition from this life to the next. We have another promise at the end of the age. A promise that stands through eternity, even though the Earth and Heavens will be destroyed and remade! *"Now the dwelling of God is with men, and he will live with them. They will be his people, and God himself will be with them and be their God.* *⁴He will wipe every tear from their eyes. There will be no more death or mourning or crying or pain, for the old order of things has passed away."*²

Furthermore, the answer to the question, "What happens to a believer when they die?" is not as simple as, "They go to Heaven." As we study the prophetic passages of the Bible, we learn about the amazing adventure that is set before us as we rule and reign with Christ. The salvation that we now have is only in part. But in the future, more of our salvation will be realized as we take part in the resurrection of our bodies, the rewarding of the saints, the millennial reign of Christ, Satan's final doom, and observation of the New Heavens and New Earth being wonderfully created as our eternal dwelling!

We are serving the Lord because we love him first and foremost. But we are also serving him because of what he has promised us in our future. If you have been serving the Lord to avoid going to hell, I hope that this book has moved you into a new relationship with God. A relationship that is motivated not by fear, but by love, adventure, and promise! If you have been serving the Lord because you think that godliness will make you successful, wealthy or significant in this life, I hope that this time spent in reading has pressed your gaze forward. We are not living for this life; we are living for the next. Pride, lust, and greed often try to pull my gaze off of heaven and back to the positions, wealth, pleasure, and influence of this life. Let's keep our eyes on the goal, our Savior Jesus Christ and trust that our best life is yet to come! The Word of God is full of instruction, guidance and encouragement for life here on earth. If you choose to study and continue to learn, it also carries many hints about how we will live then, and what lies ahead for the believer after this life.

---

[1] Matthew 28:20
[2] Revelation 21:3-4

LaVergne, TN USA
04 March 2011
218909LV00002B/22/P